This book is a game changer for the way you see yourself and connect with the world. Nicole's wisdom will help you take your relationships and your life to the next level. Miracles are waiting for you!

ALLI WORTHINGTON, bestselling author, speaker, and business coach

We all know that one conversation we really should have but don't. We sabotage the relationships that could be most fulfilling and impactful because we don't know how to say what needs to be said. Nicole provides wise perspective and a practical approach to engaging in difficult conversations that are balanced with truth and grace—a powerful combination we often forget to use.

STEVE PERKINS, founder and CEO of Greenhouse Culture

With solid advice and practical phrases to use in the middle of any argument, *The Miracle Moment* does exactly what it suggests: gives you the power to make miracles happen in your relationships.

ELISA MORGAN, author, speaker, and cohost of the *God Hears Her* podcast

Navigating conflict is an essential tool as long as you are dealing with human beings, yet most people don't prepare and practice for conflict! Nicole has masterfully given us a start-to-finish practical guide for navigating the inevitable.

DAVID M. BAILEY, coauthor of the *Race, Class, and the Kingdom of God* study series

As you walk into a room of hard questions and tough conversations, Nicole invites you closer to see where grace exists. Her honesty and pursuit of truth refresh your soul and give you hope.

ERYN EDDY, founder of So Worth Loving lifestyle company and author of *So Worth Loving: How Discovering Your True Value Changes Everything*

Nicole has artfully distilled her experience as therapist, coach, and pastor into a chairside companion designed to help you navigate conflict with integrity while setting and holding boundaries. The book is a treasure of stories and exercises designed to resolve dilemmas. Nicole has been a blessing in my career with her ability to reframe/reconsider situations, and her expertise shines through in this book.

JOSEPH BOWERS, CEO of The CREATiON Companies

The Miracle Moment is a miracle indeed. Nicole Unice has created the ultimate guide for navigating tough conversations. As a woman over forty, I've had more tough discussions than I can count. Often I've avoided people and conversations out of "kindness," never knowing just how unkind my actions were. Nicole's introduction and step-by-step guide to identifying our intentions and feelings prior to speaking is a game changer. After devouring Nicole's new body of work, I'm armed with a plan and all I need to restore past relationships and future roadblocks.

AMEERAH SAINE, host of the *Brunch and Slay* podcast

Too many leaders underestimate the importance of tough conversations. They either avoid them or they insensitively barrel through them, blind to their own feelings and motivations, and often completely unaware of the impact on the relationships in their lives. Nicole's experience as a counselor, pastor, and coach powerfully equips you with the tools to have healthy and honest conversations that lead to true miracle moments.

JENNI CATRON, author, leadership coach, and founder of The 4Sight Group

As a counselor, one of the greatest needs I see in my clients is the desire for deep, life-giving conversations. Ironically, we often feel the need for this type of communication in the hard places of pain and conflict—the very places where we are most tempted to withdraw from one another. Each chapter in *The Miracle Moment* is full of concrete teaching, engaging illustrations, and practical steps of application to help us move toward tough conversations with the people close to us. These tools can help us have more authentic conversations that will strengthen, rather than destroy, our most meaningful relationships.

LISA G. OULD, counselor and executive director of The Barnabas Center–Richmond

The most challenging spaces in life and leadership are relationships. In this must-read for leaders everywhere, Nicole Unice delivers a just-in-time, practical pathway to navigate the conversations we dread most. Nicole's unique ability to weave timeless wisdom with relevant stories provides a relatable and powerful tool for leaders in every walk of life.

GABRIEL SMITH, founder and CEO of 3rd Source

Nicole Unice gives us the principles and tools we need to navigate the challenge of living in healthy relationships. Yet *The Miracle Moment* is so vulnerable, honest, and relevant that once you've read it, you'll want to keep it close (for regular reference) so you stay positioned for more miracle moments in your life. This book would be relevant in the White House, not to mention boardrooms, offices, churches, kitchen tables, bedrooms, backyards, and front porches!

PASTOR DON COLEMAN, lead pastor of East End Fellowship and former chairman of the Richmond, Virginia, public school board

When many of us think about miracle moments, it's usually through the lens of something happening to us. What I love about Nicole's approach and coaching style is that she has witnessed how important it is for *leaders* to move in order for miracle moments to happen. We can't just sit back and wait for them. Miracles happen when we look inside and put ourselves in position to experience them!

TYLER REAGIN, founder of the Life-Giving Company and cofounder of the 10TEN Project

The Miracle Moment teaches us how to think, feel, and react in an honest and vulnerable way. Nicole's insight into becoming a non-anxious presence can be a life-changing tool for self-awareness. Through this book, you will discover you have the courage to be an open and honest person in all your relationships.

DR. CHRIS PAYNE, senior pastor of New City Church, Charlotte, North Carolina

In *The Miracle Moment*, Nicole invites us to pay attention to what is going on within us and to be curious, not condemning. She gives us tools that anyone can use and lets us know that there is hope in Jesus. And she cheers us on the whole way. There is more for all of us!

KATINA NAPPER, strategic leader, consultant, and coach

With her discernment as a pastor and her experience as a counselor, Nicole is the coach you want in your corner. Her book will help you see what you're missing when you shrink from difficult conversations and show you how to press in for the miracle moment waiting on the other side. If you want to thrive in your life and leadership, let this practical book guide the way to transforming your relationships.

JULIE PIERCE, leadership coach, author, and speaker

THE MIRACLE MOMENT

How Tough
Conversations Can
Actually Transform
Your Most Important
Relationships

NICOLE UNICE

TYNDALE
MOMENTUM®

The Tyndale nonfiction imprint

∿∿∿∿

To each person represented by the stories in this book—your lives have deeply impacted my understanding of love, commitment, and relationships. You make me believe in miracles.

∿∿∿∿

Table of Contents

MIRACLES STILL HAPPEN

IT WAS THE LAST SENTENCE that caught my attention.

I had met Sam less than an hour before in my work with a nonprofit trying to move their culture from "scrappy startup" to an established and locally respected organization. When I'd arrived at our meeting place, a coffee shop run by the organization's leadership development program, Sam was already waiting. He quickly stood, drink in hand, to greet me with a firm handshake. We found a table in the corner, away from the relaxed chatter between baristas and customers. Once we sat down, I could tell by his tight smile and straight posture that this wouldn't be an easy assignment.

I wasn't surprised—Sam was the organization's director of operations and had been through a tumultuous staff shake-up. Their founding executive director had left under pressure more than a year before, and about a third of the program team had resigned since then. I had already spent hours interviewing all of Sam's coworkers on the central team, and their tension and pain were palpable. It was the last sentence in my conversation with Sam that unlocked the crux of the problem.

My first order of business had been just to listen to Sam's story. In all my conversations, I'd been searching for a way forward—and trying to identify those staff members who seemed willing to engage with the hard work of rebuilding a team. I wanted to make sure I got under the surface and understood each person's heart. I quieted my thoughts, focused on Sam, and said, "So, tell me your story of coming into this role."

Sam flashed a brief smile and folded his hands in front of him, knee jiggling to a silent rhythm under the table. "Well, my story is pretty important to my work here—I was one of the kids this program served when I was in middle school. I never thought I could use my business background to actually work for a mission I believe in . . ." He trailed off, the smile fading. "I still believe in what we are doing here. But sometimes I'm not sure the executive team know exactly what they are doing."

With his coffee untouched, Sam leaned in and paused, squeezing his interlaced fingers together. But once he began to speak, I wasn't sure he would be able to stop. It seemed as if Sam hadn't really felt heard in years, and was about to finally open up.

He filled me in on more of his background: He'd been on staff for eight years, often feeling trapped by the tension between the front-facing program for the community and the actual business of the organization. For years he'd been navigating the turbulent environment—before the executive director left and during the leadership vacuum afterward. Meanwhile, his responsibilities kept expanding, but his pay and hours stayed the same. He was understandably exhausted and frustrated. Over the next hour, he talked about his work, about inconsistencies in the direction of the organization, and especially about his department's supervisor, Abby.

By the time the deluge of words slowed to a trickle, Sam had stopped jiggling his knee and now cupped his cold coffee. He sighed deeply, then lifted his fingers from his drink, a half-hearted gesture of surrender.

"When Abby told my team, 'If you can't get on board, you might as well get going,' I thought, *Are you kidding me? This is not the way a leader leads. You can't say that to people, even if that's what you mean. If something doesn't change, I don't know how much longer I can last.*"

I don't know how much longer I can last. That's the sentence that caught my attention because it expresses the very human moment in difficult circumstances when we must decide whether to power up or give up—and Sam had just revealed that he had reached that breaking point.

Throughout our time together, Sam had brought up Abby repeatedly. He had a long relationship with her—she had been his program director when he first came on as a high school volunteer, and he had celebrated her rise in leadership. Abby had now been with the organization almost fifteen years and was the leader with the most seniority. She had always been an important voice in Sam's life, but for the last eighteen months, Sam felt he could no longer trust her in the same way.

He told me about the day he encouraged the development director to voice a concern on behalf of the team and Abby "just never responded." And there was the time that Sam's (now-fired) manager reassured him, after he'd put in sixty-hour weeks for months, that Abby would advocate for a position to give Sam more leadership and relief from the day-to-day grind. Lowering his head, Sam told me, "I was so disappointed that she didn't do anything." And then Sam was crushed when Abby seemed to throw him under the bus in a meeting. He wondered whether working so hard—even for an organization he believed in so passionately—was worth it anymore.

I wanted Abby to be the problem, I really did. By this point, I knew Sam was a well-regarded, hardworking staff member. I understood Sam's frustration and his belief that all his team needed was to find Abby a better place in the organization and to hire an *experienced* executive. We often believe that by re-engineering job titles and positions, we can fix a workplace, but that kind of problem-solving usually doesn't deal with the real issue—our own humanity. And before we can deal with all that "humanity" around us, we have to deal with ourselves. After just one hour with Sam, I had a hunch that he had let his anger and frustration lead him to the conclusion that the problem was Abby. But I wondered how the story might play out differently if Sam understood how to explore what was driving his frustration—and what steps he could take to reshape his experience.

To make matters more interesting, I had spent time with Abby and the executive team the day before. I found her to be a passionate (albeit tired) and committed leader who wanted to do right and had more than enough experience to lead the organization forward. Abby was bearing just as much emotional weight as Sam—no surprise there—but she was carrying it behind the scenes. She had to manage ongoing tensions among the executive team and a difficult relationship with the current board, who seemed more interested in sabotaging and second-guessing her efforts than actually moving forward. She was also worried about her oldest son, a junior in high school, who had recently decided he wasn't into school—or anything other than mumbling and staring into his phone. Abby had admitted to me (and was completely embarrassed for "being so unprofessional") that she had found a marijuana stash in her son's room for the second time in a month and couldn't get her husband to engage with what felt like a red-alert problem in their home. Abby was flailing—trying to act as if she had it all together while her life was tearing apart at the seams.

"I thought I worked well with people," she told me, "but right now it seems like all I have are more and more people with bigger and bigger problems."

As in tune as Abby seemed to be, I was surprised at her response when I questioned her about the morale on the rest of the staff. "Things are good. I can depend on my team, and they do awesome work. I haven't been as engaged these last few months, but they know what to do and are doing a great job handling the changes."

Now, having talked with both Sam and Abby, I felt like I was watching a train wreck. I understood how they had both derailed, and I was empathetic to both. Certainly, when considering their relationship, it's crucial to remember how the power differential between them played a role. Yet Sam did have the choice to confront Abby—but chose not to. Unbeknownst to Abby, Sam was carrying firsthand experiences and secondhand gossip about Abby that had damaged his trust and soured his view of her—but he hadn't yet acknowledged that growing tension within him. Conversely, Abby had chosen to grit it out under the weight of her work and personal challenges, and yet she had blind spots to serious issues that were eroding her most important asset: her relational influence and trust with her staff.

As I sat down to write my assessment, I realized that the entire team was at a critical crossroad. If they continued on the current trajectory—burying hurts, avoiding confrontation, sidestepping honest and vulnerable relationships—they were in for a world of pain. That kind of distress comes in the form of emotional baggage for people who leave the organization, continued frustration for those who stay, and more than anything, the incredible missed opportunity to grow, to flourish, and ultimately to serve the nonprofit's mission more effectively and passionately.

If their situation was left unchecked, I was certain this is exactly what would eventually happen to Sam and Abby. Yet I also knew the fallout from the stress and hurt on both sides could be avoided. If they were willing to acknowledge and confront their frustration and disappointment, they would strengthen their department and, I was sure, find their work much more satisfying. This could be a miracle moment.

What was happening between Sam and Abby—and what is happening between coworkers, best friends, husbands and wives, and parents and their adult children—is human. It's the struggle to express what's going on within us, to confront misunderstandings and mistakes, to align our words and our actions in a way that allows us to be open, vulnerable, and courageous when a relationship isn't going well.

The problem is, most of us have never learned how to handle conflict, so our relationships tend to be superficial, transactional, and often unfulfilling. But it doesn't have to be like this for Sam, for Abby, or for you. There is another way.

Too often, though, we overlook and even run away from the pivotal moments that could change everything. After all, these interactions are fraught with difficulties, and miracle moments happen only when we refuse to back away from uncomfortable truth. They bring with them the possibility of failure, the missteps, and the inevitable awkwardness that come when you try to relate in a new way after being stuck in a pattern for a while. Yet these conversations are also the one route that can lead to renewed relationships and lasting change.

Let's Deal with It

We often have a feeling that something isn't right but can't identify what is at the root of our discomfort. Perhaps, like Sam, you have struggled with that frustrated, irritated, unsettled feeling you have when you want someone to understand you—and he or she is just not getting it. You may have experienced a vague sense that something is "off" with someone but don't have the words to express your concern and reconnect with that person. Or maybe, like Abby, you wish you had a better connection, better camaraderie, a better sense of "getting" your child or someone else you love but figure you must settle for what is.

Since most of us were never taught how to speak openly and directly with someone about how we feel, what we are experiencing, and how to move forward in a relationship, such struggles shouldn't be surprising. If you'd like to better navigate such difficulties, you've come to the right place.

I've spent the last twenty years as a therapist, pastor, and coach, helping people change the way they understand themselves and one another. In this book, we'll explore some of the issues we all face in conflict, like how to

- name the feelings that are driving your decisions and actions,
- learn to respect and respond to your emotions without letting them control you,
- identify the emotional triggers that set you off—and sabotage your relationships,
- get a conversation back on track when it's gone sideways,
- speak words that help—rather than hurt—the likelihood of your getting what you need,
- avoid having the same argument over and over,
- navigate a conflict with integrity,
- mend a relationship when you think you've blown it,
- decide whether to confront an issue or let it go,
- identify and keep yourself safe from toxic people, and
- become comfortable setting and holding boundaries.

Throughout the book, you'll find stories and exercises designed to help you resolve these dilemmas. I've learned so much from the people I've worked with, but even more from my own human experience, trying to navigate the tricky situations of marriage, parenting, and leadership. In trying to understand the environment that gives me and you the courage to change, I've put my relationships and experiences under the microscope. In the process, I've stumbled over my inability to hold healthy boundaries, to confront issues as they arise, to find the real problems that get in the way of trust and respect. I've ignored every piece of advice I've ever tried to give other people—I'm stubborn like that.

Yet even when I've failed miserably at important conversations, interpreting my feelings, or speaking my mind gently but firmly, I haven't given up hope that change is possible. You see, I believe in miracles. I'll unpack what I mean when I talk about miracle moments in chapter 1, but for now, it's enough to know that these opportunities come in the very second when your frustration, hurt, or rejection makes you want to disengage—but you lean in instead. They exist in the unexpected space between two people trying to express themselves, trying to be understood and loved. They reveal themselves in moments of active listening, mutual compromise, and real apologies.

So if you want to do your relationships better, consider this book the best kind of therapy—it's cheap, it's available when you are, and you can take it at your own pace. Not only do I believe that we can all learn to relate in ways that will transform our relationships, I believe in a God who is orchestrating miracles designed to convince you of His love and grace. But whether you go to church, have been burned by church, aren't interested in church, or fall somewhere in-between, you are welcome here. The principles apply regardless of your own spiritual journey. *The Miracle Moment DVD Experience* and participant's guide take a deep dive into ways Jesus modeled and lived into relationships, and if this book piques your interest in that, I invite you to work through both of them as well.

Miracle moments require true vulnerability, as well as the willingness to express yourself clearly and allow yourself to be truly seen. You can make a choice to keep that troublesome relationship small and irritating—to keep giving up, shutting up, or blowing up—or you can step into the space where miracles happen. It won't happen every time or with everyone. It may cost you, as not everyone will be willing to change with you. But I believe in the power of miracle moments. And I believe there are miracles waiting for you.

CHAPTER 1

FIGHTING FOR A MIRACLE

∧∧∧∧∧∧

Wounds from a sincere friend are better
than many kisses from an enemy.

PROVERBS 27:6

LOOKING BACK, I knew we were breaking every civility rule when we brought up politics. We were out celebrating my friend's birthday. I don't know why we started talking about the upcoming election. I don't remember who brought it up (it was probably me), but I do know that what had been a lovely dinner at a white-tablecloth restaurant devolved quickly from a heated conversation about policy into a personal conflict involving accusations like "You make me feel stupid" and "You are so stubborn."

Happy birthday, everyone!

By the time the birthday girl and I had returned to that polite iciness that covers friendship when words have gone too far, our other friend was hiding out in the bathroom. Sure that I had lost two best friends, my insecurity was on full alert. How had "productive" dialogue turned into a weapons of mass destruction–level conflict before we had even ordered dessert?

When was the last time you had a fight like this, one that led to inner turmoil because you felt unheard, judged, or disregarded? Perhaps your argument didn't end in verbal sparring. It might have happened entirely within your head because—once you sensed that you were being deeply misunderstood—you used silence and withdrawal to protect yourself. Perhaps you've been in the kind of spat where both sides launch a volley of conflicting opinions and then walk away. Or maybe you've been in a conversation that ends with one person lecturing and the other withdrawing.

Many of us have never actually had a *good* fight. We've never experienced a struggle that ended in healing and strength—for us or the other party. Rather than engaging with the person who has hurt or disappointed us, we've just sucked it up, stuffed it away, or distanced ourselves, perhaps believing that there's something inherently wrong with us or that it's just not possible to really be honest and still be loved.

When I think about what it takes to communicate openly and honestly, to move toward connection, to grab hold of a miracle moment, I think *fight* is the right word to use. The basic definition of a fight is "a violent struggle involving weapons." You might be thinking, *Really? I thought good relationships are all about harmony and selflessness. What's the miracle in that?*

We all want to be known and accepted just as we are, but no one can do that perfectly. The violence comes in the form of the invisible but powerful struggle to be known and to know others. The weapons come in the form of words—words you choose, words you use, and words you withhold.

This battle is fought on two fronts. The first is the obvious one. It's the struggle you have to be understood by your spouse, your kids, your annoying coworker, or your pretentious neighbor. Jessica, for example, came to me because she was contemplating divorce. She insisted that she and her husband never fought. I politely nodded and kept a poker face, but I was thinking, *Yes, you do; you just don't know it yet.* Neither she nor her husband was keeping a big secret, like an affair or secret addiction, from the other. As we talked, I realized that though she and her husband might not yell, they did use withholding affection and information from each other as weapons. Though they didn't insult each other verbally, they withdrew from each other—seldom sharing what they were really thinking and feeling. They weren't growing together through the challenges of life—building careers, parenting young children, keeping up their home. No, they didn't *fight.*

But maybe they should have.

These are the obvious battles. But there's much more.

The second front is more insidious—and more deadly. It's the battlefront of the conversation you have among others and within yourself. Every day, we talk to the people closest to us: spouses, kids, coworkers, bosses. At the same time, each of us carries on a dialogue with ourselves in our minds.

Drew, a talented, up-and-coming leader, came to me for coaching as he considered a big career change. He was having difficulty figuring out what he wanted and was paralyzed by the choices in front of him. Midway through our work together, I gave him homework to help him see his decisions more clearly. When we met to discuss the assignment, he confessed he hadn't done it. I asked him to be curious (something we will practice later in this book) and be an impartial observer of himself to consider the reason he had put it off.

"So, Drew," I said, "what kept you from actually following through and doing what you said you would do?" I sat quietly. A big part of me wanted to let Drew off the hook and rescue him from his own mistake, but I had a feeling that the real miracle would be missed if I didn't allow this uncomfortable interaction to move us forward.

The silence was obviously difficult for Drew. He began to struggle—and not just to find words. He actually began to squirm slightly, raising his shoulders and jiggling his knees. It was like watching the 1986 movie *Aliens*. I half-expected a foreign creature to burst from his chest. At one point he tapped his own head with his palm. "I don't know what's wrong with me!" he said, his eyes down. "I don't know why I think I can handle more responsibility when I keep messing up!" Apparently when I'd asked him to consider why he hadn't completed his homework, I had stepped on a buried land mine neither one of us knew was there. I suspected that Drew's procrastination in a little thing like homework was related to a much bigger thing that had greater ramifications for his life—fear of discovering that he feels inadequate inside, fear of failing, fear of not measuring up. Drew's battle may be invisible and internal, but it's just as real as Jessica's, Sam's, and Abby's.

One of the greatest joys in life is the ability to experience freedom and connection with ourselves and each other. But the only path to freedom is engaging in the struggle to express what's inside of us, outside of us. In a rare moment of vulnerability, Drew, a successful, highly relational leader, allowed me in on the conversation in his head—the very powerful words that were keeping him from moving into his future. And though he didn't realize it, the misalignment between his accomplishments and his self-perception affected the way he related to those closest to him as well as those who could help him advance in his career. A similar disconnect between their inner thoughts and interactions with each other is impacting Sam's desire to stay in his job and Abby's ability to retain her team's trust.

> The only path to freedom is engaging in the struggle to express what's inside of us, outside of us.

Most of us experience a one-two punch of pain when we feel overlooked or misunderstood. The first jab is a sense of being overwhelmed at our inability to communicate clearly. And then the knockout punch:

the shame we feel because we assume we should know how to navigate our relationships by now. Rather than growing in our ability to express ourselves and our needs, to honor our emotions, and to mature into the people we want to become, we shut down or lash out, resulting in even more pain. Rather than becoming more vulnerable and resilient, we decide we are essentially broken, unworthy, and incapable of being fully known and fully loved. This is a lonely place—having the gift of language but struggling mightily to use it.

I get it. Not only have I spent the last twenty years helping people find the words they need for this two-fronted battle, but I know the fluttery, clammy-hand feeling of staring down a confrontation personally. I know the agony of trying—and failing—to express what I truly mean to a loved one. I know that delicate moment of decision when I can choose to speak vulnerably in my search for a connection and risk rejection, or I can decide to land the verbal sucker punch that will make me feel clever and justified in the moment. Though 100 percent of us will have conflict, only the brave few will use it as the training ground that leads to a deeper, more meaningful life together.

These courageous souls will recognize and seize the miracle moment: the moment in a conversation when you want to shut up, give up, or blow up—and you lean in instead. It's not the moment you react to being hurt, misunderstood, or treated unfairly. It's the moment after the initial reaction, when you change course and respond differently.

MIRACLE MOMENT: The moment in a conversation when you want to shut up, give up, or blow up—and you lean in instead. It's not the moment you react to being hurt, misunderstood, or treated unfairly. It's the moment after the initial reaction, when you change course and respond differently.

The plan is simple—but I'll warn you: Simple doesn't mean easy. Long-held patterns of thinking don't disappear overnight, and learning new skills takes time. But you can move from overwhelmed and underprepared to confident and skilled in even the toughest conversations.

This book is divided into three parts designed to help you move inward for insight and then outward for impact. Part 1 will help you gain self-awareness as you discover how your emotions and thoughts work together, and how you can learn to recognize and respond appropriately to your emotions. We'll spend most of our time in part 2, where we will learn about self-expression. If you've ever felt woefully underprepared to handle a conflict, if you've felt like your words either don't work or work in overdrive, getting you into trouble, this section will be invaluable. We'll break down the mechanics of how to engage in a conflict, move toward reconciliation and compromise, and rebuild trust after it's been broken. Part 3 is on self-respect—making sure your actions line up with your words so you live with integrity, even in those times when you feel as if you've failed.

As we begin, I encourage you to think about a relationship that you want to improve. Take a moment to visualize what you would like to experience with that person. Do you wish your roommate understood you better? Do you long for deeper connection or intimacy in your marriage? Can you picture a constructive conversation in which you are able to be your full self and express your needs? Can you imagine deeper respect between you as you hear and learn from each other's perspectives?

Keep that visual in mind as you begin your work here so that your learning remains grounded in real life. You won't do it perfectly, but you will make progress. That's the incredible thing about being human: We are flawed, but we are never finished.

CHAPTER 2

THE MAKING OF
A MIRACLE

∧∧∧∧

"Actions speak louder than words" is a lie.
Nothing speaks louder than when our words match our
meaning and our meaning matches our actions.

IF YOU WANT TO KNOW whether change is hard, try crossing your arms the opposite way.

Try writing your name with your nondominant hand.

Try lacing up the "other" shoe first.

We are all creatures of habit. We have patterns of living and relating that have been built and reinforced over time. The great thing about habits is that they are *efficient*. If you've ever driven from home to work with no memory of how the drive actually took place, then you've experienced the efficiency of your brain going on autopilot. Such routines prevent the inevitable decision-making fatigue that would come if we had to make thousands of choices each day. By building habits, our brains conserve energy for more important matters (like deciding where to eat out for lunch).

But here's the problem: Actions prompted by habits and actions driven by goals compete for the same brain circuitry.[1] If you are acting out of habit, when your goals try to call in, they are going to find the line busy. Not only that, but much like writing with your non-dominant hand, acting on new goals often feels awkward and clunky compared to the smooth sailing of a habit.

Now take all of this truth and apply it to emotionally charged situations.

If you have ever returned to your childhood home for a holiday, you know that strange but universal experience of regressing immediately to your teenage self, regardless of your chronological age. You walk into a house that reminds you of what you experienced (or lacked) as a child, and the next thing you know, you are exchanging insults with your brother over the backgammon board and rolling your eyes at your mother while stomping through the kitchen.

Oliver Burkeman defines this "holiday tradition" as "the ferocious black hole that sucks adult children, and their parents, back into family roles from years or even decades ago, the moment they've reassembled under one roof."[2] Regardless of how much you believe you've grown and how much you pump yourself up to be good before you turn into that familiar neighborhood, the powerful nature of habits means the phone line that is your brain is ringing busy when you try to move toward different actions.

Just as our early years imprint us with powerful reactions to the dynamics of our family, as adults we take our habitual actions (and reactions) into our workplaces, our friendships, and our homes. If we aren't aware of how our inner habits of relating impact what we do, we end up frustrated and insecure. We have no knowledge of how our words or reactions are helping—or hurting—our ability to get what we want. And even when we do sense that our actions and reactions aren't getting the desired results, the power of the habit is so strong that the goal-directed side of our brain has trouble breaking in.

The bad news: This is true of every single one of us, no matter how idyllic our family life or how blissful our adult circumstances.

The good news: This is true of every single one of us, which means your spouse, your boss, your parent, and your coworker all have similar struggles.

A little more bad news: Only those who are brave enough to try to be different ever succeed. Deciding it's worth the work is a personal decision that you can't make for anyone else. This journey has to be, first and foremost, about you.

A lot more good news: There is a universal truth at play here: If you change, everything and everyone around you will change.

If you've spent time with anyone over the age of seventy, you probably have witnessed a best-case and worst-case example of this. Every one of us knows a bitter, lonely old person—and hopefully you also know a joyful, peaceful one. The difference lies right here: *The way we grow is not about just changing—it's about aligning **what we feel** with **what we think** and **how we act.***

When my daughter was eleven and training as a high-level gymnast, she suffered a stress fracture in her back. As a result, she had to wear a brace for twelve weeks and then rehabilitate with physical therapy for months. During her recovery, we discovered that her right leg was slightly shorter than her left. The disparity created extra torque on her back and stressed other parts of her body, from her hips to her shoulders. This imbalance, combined with the advanced twisting movements she was practicing, created the fracture.

Of course, it seemed obvious to me that the treatment was to align her legs. I imagined that a special shoe lift could make the necessary adjustment, although the thought of her dealing with an insert in every shoe for the rest of her life wasn't very appealing.

And although shoe lifts might be best in some cases, for her, the right approach turned out to be allowing her body to move into alignment on its own. She was still growing, and if we had tricked her body into thinking her legs were aligned, it would not have known how to develop properly.

Over the next three years, she grew several inches and retired from gymnastics. After her back healed, X-rays showed that she had healthy spacing in her discs and joints. Her body then did what we hoped it would do: Her legs evened out, and the rest of her body did as well. Over time, focusing on *alignment* is what created lasting and healthy growth.

Just as shoe lifts seemed like a quick fix early in our ordeal, so you may want a fast-acting formula to make your husband finally listen to you, your teenager respect you, and your boss advocate for you. Instead, we'll be turning the mirror on ourselves. Rather than dealing with tools and techniques that change us, we are going to look at ourselves from the perspective of alignment: How can I mean what I feel, say what I mean, and do what I say in every situation? This kind of alignment creates integrity, a word with the same root as the word *integrate*.

Integrity comes when we process our emotions, communicate with truth and love, and follow through with our actions. It's the holistic expression of our heart, mind, and strength aligning in the way we move through the world. Our integrity is tested and shaped as we experience our life with others, one conversation at a time. But achieving this alignment takes work, and it's often right in the normal stuff of life that we discover what integrity really looks like in us.

ALIGNMENT:

I mean what I feel;

I say what I mean;

I do what I say.

Alignment in Action

My phone vibrated. Recognizing the number of my younger coworker and friend, I smiled and answered.

"Hey, Brent, what's up?" I turned my face to the sunshine and closed my eyes. I was in the stands watching my son play soccer—although I was more excited about being out in the beautiful weather than about watching the third game of the weekend.

Brent spoke hesitantly. "I really hate to bother you on a Saturday . . ."

"Brent, you are not bothering me. If I were busy, I wouldn't have answered. What's going on?"

He paused for a moment. "I feel so dumb needing help with this, but I . . . need to say no to Sarah's invitation and I don't know how." I smiled again, not because I was happy that Brent was feeling angsty about Sarah, but because I enjoy helping my friends sort out their feelings so they can align them with the actions they need to take in their relationships.

Brent had recently started dating Sarah, who had asked him to accompany her to her sister's wedding out of town. I knew that Brent had only recently discovered the importance of establishing healthy boundaries. We had chatted about the wedding invitation over lunch earlier in the week, so I was caught up on the scenario.

"OK," I responded, "let's talk about what you really want to say."

My conversation on the soccer field represents thousands of other conversations I've had with people over the years. People trying to make a connection. People trying to confront an issue. People trying to say no. People trying to say yes. These dilemmas are not "dumb" or inconsequential. They are actually quite difficult, as anyone who's ever had to disappoint someone, break up with someone, apologize to someone, or confront someone can tell you.

But the uncomfortable friction we feel in such situations is the place where we can experience change. Brent wasn't just trying to figure out how to say no to Sarah. He was trying to learn how to bring what was inside of him outside—stumbling through the scary world of expressing himself to someone else.

What Calculus Taught Me about the School of Life

Let me illustrate what it takes to pursue alignment through a story of learning (and the worst student/teacher interaction of my school career). I want you to meet my math professor, whom I'll call Dr. Eraser. He didn't just teach calculus; he literally helped write the book on it (those of you who've suffered through *Multivariable Calculus* know it well). Dr. Eraser taught my first (and last) college math class for many reasons, mostly having to do with this story.

As much as I'd like to put it behind me, I can clearly picture my regular seat in his classroom. I was a college freshman who thought a lot more about the cute boy who sat in front of me than about derivative functions. In my defense, Dr. Eraser made it easy for my mind to wander. He would put his nose two inches from the chalkboard and talk directly into it for the better part of fifty minutes, rarely turning around. He would write such long formulas on the board that he would erase with one hand while writing with the other. I barely copied down the beginning of the problem before he had moved on.

With every passing class, I realized how little I knew about calculus—and about college in general. And Dr. Eraser didn't do much to make it OK to not be OK at math. As I struggled, my mind began to worry: If I was so woefully unprepared for this class . . . maybe I was on the verge of failing every other class too. With no confidence and no real plan on how to improve, I limped through calculus and barely muscled out a low C. (But I did marry the cute boy who sat in front of me, so all was not lost.)

The beautiful thing about being a grown-up is that we have agency over many of our choices, which means I actually didn't have to use calculus *ever* again. But what I've realized over the years is that if it is hard to admit when you need help with transcendental functions (what does that even mean?), it's even harder to admit that you need help being a person.

One reason Dr. Eraser was the world's worst calculus teacher (sorry, my C- still stings . . .) is that math came so easily to him. As a result, he flew through the fundamental steps—leaving me in the (chalk?) dust. He may have excelled in calculus, but he could have used a little help on the human side.

Dr. Eraser seemed to have an innate grasp of calculus skills, but most of us don't come by people skills naturally. What we assume is intuitive and easy for some people has actually been hard-won and honed over time. No one is born with impeccable emotional intelligence and empathy. No teenager is an artful and nuanced conflict resolver—and most adults aren't either. Nobody is great, at first, with understanding their inner world and knowing how to harness thoughts and emotions into words that make sense to other people—or even themselves. If you want an example of how hard it is to control your emotions and make sense of them, spend time with a three-year-old! Because the way we react and respond to emotions, to other people, and to hurt feels so automatic, changing the way we relate to others and to ourselves isn't just dramatic—it's a miracle.

The real miracle is in becoming our full selves, living with courage and vulnerability and integrity. In her book *Big Magic*, author Elizabeth Gilbert writes, "The universe buries strange jewels deep within us all, and then stands back to see if we can find them."[3] Seizing the miracle moments in our relationships is about stepping back and discovering that they've been available to us all along.

The Five Laws of Miracles

I want to introduce you to a surprising set of principles that drive relationships. These laws are counterintuitive and often clash with the conflict-survival skills we've developed, and they take courage and effort to embrace. The following five laws sum up what I've learned about how we can make positive change in our lives. These are the beliefs we must cling to before we can accept ourselves, grow into our full potential, and relate to others with freedom and truth.

Law #1: Nice is bad

Remember Brent's struggle to figure out how to say no to Sarah's invitation? One of the reasons Brent was having such a hard time declining the out-of-town wedding invitation was because he was obsessed with being nice. For Brent, that meant not rocking the boat, not disappointing anyone ever, and most certainly not giving a solid no to anything. The problem is, this version of "nice" isn't nice at all. Although kind is good, loving is good, truth is good—nice is bad. In fact, when the word *nice* came into the English language five hundred years ago, it meant "foolish," "stupid," "ignorant."[4] Just goes to show how far a word can come!

When someone describes another person as nice, I assume they mean he or she is somewhere between OK and boring. Nice is fine for the pleasantries we exchange at the grocery store or on the subway, but it lacks the rigor and resilience real relationships require. Nice is good for acquaintances but is *no good* when it keeps us from expressing our needs, pursuing real reconciliation, or asserting our boundaries. Choosing nice over honest, vulnerable, or true is bad—because it robs people of your true self.

I knew Brent well enough to see that his "nice" was getting in the way of his best. I had experienced one of its effects myself—a quiet doubt that had crept into our work together. Because I knew Brent was too "nice" to say no, I never really knew if his yes was sincere. I would often second-guess our conversations because I wasn't sure if he was telling me the truth or if he was just trying to spare my feelings. And because of that, I found myself hoping that Brent believed me when I said he wasn't bothering me by calling during my son's soccer game—but I couldn't be sure.

Nice had become the enemy of integrity for Brent, and he was struggling mightily to get past it.

I ended up describing this problem to Brent on the phone as "the Nice Disorder."

People who suffer from the Nice Disorder aren't less angry or assertive or needy than other people. They are just less willing to acknowledge it, which means their needs often come out sideways in the form of passive-aggressiveness, simmering resentment, or isolating behaviors. Eventually, those with unacknowledged needs may even begin to cope through escapism behaviors in the "over" category: overeating, overdrinking, overshopping, overNetflixing.

Without intervention, this consistent pattern of subjugating one's own needs to meet the needs of others can lead to depression, anxiety, or physical illness.[5] The good news is that this disorder is completely curable. The first step is embracing *law #1: Nice is bad*. To get beyond it, Brent would have to step back from his fear of being honest with Sarah and decide that saying yes because he was too nice to say no wasn't helping anyone, including himself.

And that's the bottom line: Nice isn't

THE NICE DISORDER

Do you suffer from a Nice Disorder? Here are a few of the symptoms:

a. consistent pattern of subjugating one's own needs to meet the needs of others, often to the detriment of one's own physical, emotional, or relational needs

b. a severe aversion to the words *no; no, thank you; no, I can't do that for you;* or *no, not at this time*

c. a paralyzing fear that standing up for one's own needs or preferences will lead to immediate rejection

helping you or anyone else. It might be protecting you; it might feel good at the time; it might be polite; but polite doesn't work with intimacy. In love, in work, in life—real relationships require vulnerability, good fights, and a much more powerful kind of love than nice.

Law #2: Chaos before order

We naturally default to unhelpful behaviors in our relationships— distance instead of depth, blame instead of apologies, talking about each other and around each other rather than to each other. We are constantly interpreting our circumstances and allowing pain and pleasure to shape the things we repeat—and the things we avoid. That's why the second law of miracles is this: *Chaos before order*.

Your life is perfectly structured for your current experience. Your relationships exist in a delicate "egosystem." An egosystem is like an ecosystem, except instead of a fragile ecology, it's made up of fragile egos. You relate to family, to coworkers, to friends, and to strangers with a distinct rhythm. For some of us, that rhythm is a loud and wild dance. For others, it's a quiet and deliberate movement. But when you begin to respond differently, you upset the egosystem around you, starting with yourself.

In Brent's case, several egos hung in the balance as he considered how to respond to Sarah. If he rejected his normal rhythm (by saying "yes" now, agonizing over it for several weeks, and then finding an excuse to back out at the last minute), he would send his egosystem into complete chaos. If Brent tried a different dance than the one he'd known, he'd be deconstructing the whole system—and it would be messy, awkward, and hard.

By pursuing a "new dance," Brent would put his predictable system out of whack—with his inner dialogue, with how he treated Sarah, with what he told his friends and mom about his no, with what Sarah's ego would tell her and what she would tell her friends. And what's worse, unless he accepted the second law of miracles, the inevitable chaos and the inner discomfort and pain from hurting Sarah would only reinforce Brent's deep-held beliefs that he was fundamentally broken and incapable of finding an honest, loving relationship. That's why acknowledging *up front* that "chaos before order" is necessary is the only way forward into real and lasting transformation. "Chaos is where we are when we don't know where we are, and what we are doing when we don't know what we are doing."[6] Our egosystem expects order, so when change is needed, we must be comfortable with the uncomfortable. Geneen Roth said, "You have to be willing to be uncomfortable, enter the unknown, do things your ego doesn't want to do. You have to value being true to what you glimpse as possible—to the heart of your heart—more than you want to be right or get your own way or be comfortable."[7]

Law #3: Curious, not condemning

The practice of getting comfortable with the uncomfortable is required in order to view our lives and reactions through a lens of curiosity, not condemnation. Brent left clues about his condemning attitude toward himself when he called his request for my help "dumb." Hidden within that little word is a big problem. As long as Brent sees himself as a person who's inept at handling boundaries, he will continue to not be able to handle his boundaries.

Most of us battle an internal condemning spirit when we enter into the chaos of the unknown—when we don't know what to say, we don't know how to say it, and we aren't sure of the results. Into those feelings of chaos, our inner conversation gets louder: *This is stupid! Why haven't you figured this out by now! This isn't going to work.* And when our conversations devolve or go sideways on us, that inner voice becomes the bully on the playground, sneering, *No one will ever understand you! No one cares! You aren't worth it!* But the third law of miracles is this: *We must become curious rather than condemning about our actions.*

You have to believe it's worth discovering why that conversation with your boss makes you want to throw your laptop out your office window, why your sister can get under your skin with one sly comment, why you feel three inches tall when your kid's teacher talks to you. When we shut down the process of discovery, we cannot learn anything, and nothing shuts down our development faster than self-condemnation. In order to grow our life, we must read our life, and that includes the messy deconstruction of our emotions, thought patterns, and reactions in the tangled dynamics of relationships.

Starting with his interactions with Sarah, Brent decided to become more curious. And once his eyes were opened to his patterns (while he fought to keep shame at bay), our own friendship—his and mine—became deeper. And because we are friends who also get to work together, I was able to observe Brent's changes within different environments. As he began to see how nice had worked against him, I noticed that he came into our work meetings with an openness for feedback and an interest in how the team was perceiving him. Becoming curious about himself allowed Brent the courage he needed to actually *want* to grow. It was a small but miraculous difference.

Law #4: Small is big

What neither Brent nor I fully realized when he asked me his "dumb" question was that he was approaching a miracle moment. But miracle moments are governed by law #4: *Small is big.* Brent was paralyzed before entering into the high-stakes conversation with Sarah because he didn't think he could express himself clearly and confidently without hurting Sarah's feelings. The lack of confidence in his ability to say no meant that pulling off this conversation would be the equivalent of a backflip on the balance beam when Brent was still working on his forward roll on the floor. And when we rush into backflips with no foundation, we fail.

This is why miracle moments happen not in massive, all-at-once transformation but in small, incremental changes to our way of relating. And this kind of fine-tuning is imprinted in God's design for the world. *Small is big* plays out in our lives all the time. For instance, our bodies require water and sleep. Being even slightly dehydrated or sleep-deprived can lead to a decline in memory and an increase in depression and anxiety. And if you've been with a three-year-old who's missed his nap, you know that a little sleep deprivation can turn even the most angelic toddler into a flaming rage machine. But a little sleep—and the angel is back. *Small is big.*

On the positive side, getting even a few minutes of morning sunlight boosts levels of serotonin in your brain, the chemical correlated to a better mood. Since the 1980s, the Japanese have been studying the effects of "forest bathing" on improving the immune system, cognitive functioning, and mood.[8] Taking a walk in the woods might literally be the secret to beginning your positive transformation. *Small is big.* We may be drawn to the dramatic and quick-fix transformations of fad diets, reality shows, and lottery winners, but true change comes through small, consistent, incremental steps.

Small changes to the way we communicate yield big results in our relationships. For Brent, that meant learning to use his no *as an intentional practice* in less emotional circumstances—no to the cracked pepper at the restaurant, no to the credit card offer at Target. It wasn't that Brent wasn't able to say no to those things before, but seeing them as small steps of practice toward bigger goals made all the difference.

Law #5: Hope makes change possible

Hope is the elixir of change. Hope is a dug-down-deep sense that it is possible to experience more in this life—more joy, more connection, more excitement, and more enjoyment with the people around you.

Across studies of well-being, the virtue of hope is consistently linked to more happiness.[9] Hope allows us to try something new when we feel stuck, helpless, or overwhelmed. Hope is linked to a fundamental belief that *change is possible.* We find hope in looking beyond our daily circumstances and focusing on creating legacy, meaning, and perseverance. And although hope is not restricted to one religion or belief system, it is the desire in our spirit for more that kindles hope into the fuel that gives us energy to change.

Your connection to something beyond yourself, your engagement with the world, and your awareness of your part in life's greater story are what make change possible. I've found that the only truly transformative change in my life has come through my beliefs being uprooted, replanted, and shaped by my faith in the life and teachings of Jesus. Jesus is the one who introduces this concept of holistic, aligned love in His greatest commandment—to love God with all our heart, mind, and strength, and to love others as we love ourselves. It's this kind of aligned love that has changed things in me and around me, and that fosters hope.

Hope means that what feels broken and useless today can become powerful and helpful tomorrow. Hope means that what's messed up can be restored. Hope means that we can approach our mistakes with curiosity, persevere through the chaos, celebrate small changes, and believe in more.

Since that conversation from the soccer field, Brent has been discovering miracles all around him—and I've been one of the beneficiaries of the change. We were working on a quick turnaround project, and when I requested he finish a task by a certain date, Brent spoke up and put a boundary around when he could complete his work. It was the first time I had received his no without it being smothered in shame or apology. I told him after the fact, "I love your no. It makes me love your yes even more!"

Brent laughed and responded, "Man, I am learning so much! It's getting easier to say no because it's making me more confident in my yes. I'm starting to get into some deep stuff behind the difficulty I have saying no—it's heavy but it's worth it. I can't believe how different I feel. I feel . . . like I'm getting free."

If you'd asked Brent a year ago if things could be different, he wouldn't have believed it. He would have told you it would take a miracle for him to experience the freedom and confidence in relationships he's growing into today. But he's now committed to the process. He's approaching his life with curiosity. He's practicing his no. And these small steps are slowly, gently harmonizing his feelings, thoughts, and actions. Alignment feels good.

∿∿∿∿

Questions to Consider

1. What is your relationship with change? Do you tend to embrace it, accept it, resist it, or deny it? Consider some of the major spheres of life: family, love, career, finances, physical well-being. Are there areas where you are more or less open to change?

2. Do you suffer from the Nice Disorder, or know anyone who does? What are the drawbacks to "playing nice" in life?

3. When you think about the five laws of miracles, which are easiest for you to believe? Which one do you resist the most? Would you add any other laws to the list from your own experiences?

CHAPTER 3

POSITIONING YOURSELF FOR A MIRACLE

∿∿∿

A winner is someone who recognizes his God-given
talents, works his tail off to develop them into skills,
and uses these skills to accomplish his goals.

LARRY BIRD

SOME OF US LEARN the art of winning on the field or the track, in Little League victories, or through soccer tournament defeats. Not me. I learned the art of winning in my first job.

At the prime age of eleven, I had a burgeoning knack for fashion with absolutely no resources to my name. So I decided it was time to work. Given my lifetime experience bossing around my two younger siblings and my familiarity with the entire Babysitter's Club book series, I figured I was as ready as anyone to offer my services. I wrote a letter to the families in my neighborhood, offering my professional child development program—aka babysitting services—at one dollar an hour per kid.

Before you could say "child labor," I landed my first gig. The Reeds were a family of five who lived on the cul-de-sac next to mine. They were unruly and worldly and fun and messy. They kept sugary cereals in the pantry and TV dinners in the freezer. They had a basement where toys jumbled riotously alongside board games with most of the pieces missing and Uno cards scattered like confetti on the carpet. I was hooked. The situation was a win all around, as I had free access to the junk food in the Reeds' pantry and a dedicated TV after bedtime, and Mr. and Mrs. Reed had the cheapest child labor in the neighborhood. And they used it, all right. Virtually every weekend, they had another party to attend, and I showed up, with all the bossiness my middle-child, eleven-year-old self could muster. There was no better place to learn the art of winning than as a preteen babysitter.

My main win of every evening on the job was bedtime. Once the kids were in bed, I knew I was basically being paid to live a better life in the Reed basement than I did at home. The Reeds had store-bought cookies and every Disney movie on VHS, two things in short supply in my home. The only thing standing between me and my best life were three children not much younger than me, who had a complete dis-regard for my "authority." The only way for me to win was to figure out how they could win too—while also keeping Mr. and Mrs. Reed happy. Winning didn't look like one victor and a bunch of losers. Winning at the Reeds' house meant *everyone* needed to win.

Competition and keeping score—and the resulting winners and losers—might work on the field and the court, but it's a terrible method for winning in relationships. The joy and appeal of competition is that it's clear cut. You have a defined goal:

Put the ball through the basket—the team with the most points in forty minutes wins

Run as fast as you can—the first person to reach the mile marker wins

Kick the ball into the goal—the side with the most goals after ninety minutes wins

It's so *tempting* to believe that the same rules of winning and losing in sports apply to winning and losing in relationships. But we must think differently if we want to win in life. The quote at the start of this chapter is from an unlikely source but perfectly underscores the idea of what it takes to really win in relationships. What worked for the Celtics' Larry Bird will also work for us. As he said, winners

- recognize their God-given talents,
- work to develop them into skills, and
- use those skills to accomplish their goals.

Notice that Bird says nothing about pushing others down to come out on top. Unfortunately, we've been programmed to believe that we need to *compete* to win—including in relationships. Competing makes us believe that "winning" happens only when the other person agrees to everything we say—and likes it! This zero-sum game means there is only one victor—either I win (I get the other person to see, believe, and agree to my way) or I lose (I get anything less than that). This belief system leads to a constant posturing and jockeying for the "winning" position, which creates a tension—an "against you" pressure instead of a "for you" energy. You see this tension all the time: in coworkers vying to lead the same project by poking holes in each other's character and skills; a husband and wife exchanging subtle criticisms at a dinner party; two family members constantly talking about each other—but never talking directly to each other. The miracle of a transformed relationship—one that has the potential of both sides growing and getting what they want—won't happen in a competitive environment.

Learning the art of "winning" in relationships didn't come easily to me.

My husband, Dave, and I met when we were freshmen in

college—hardly old enough to vote, much less handle each other's hearts. But as love goes, we found one another and discovered that we would rather do life together than any other way. We were engaged by our senior year and married right after graduation. I had come to college early, which means I was barely out of my teens on our wedding day, and we were off to "adulthood" at lightning speed.

We were so unprepared for the next season. Sure, we were relatively happy, secure, and comfortable. But we had almost zero ability to pursue healthy conflict or meaningful communication. Our shared emotional intelligence level was on par with a sixth-grade boy, and our shared tolerance for uncomfortable conversations was virtually nil.

So we would avoid hard things, steaming and stewing around each other for as long as possible. But as anyone married for more than five minutes knows, marriage is a wonderful way to get acquainted with your sin. The hard topics we didn't want to talk about—or didn't know how to discuss—just kept coming up. We had to deal with what we thought about all the things we'd just assumed we were aligned on: money, sex, family, faith, work, friendships, and who was supposed to mow the lawn. We fought about everything we thought about. This is what our communication style looked like during the first two years of our marriage:

Dave stayed quiet and processed internally.

I pushed and pushed for more connection and communication. (Some call it *nagging*; I call it *coaching*.)

Dave would finally push back against my pushing, and what I received felt harsh, critical, and unloving.

I responded with defensiveness, demands, and self-righteousness.

He would go quiet again, or offer an apology to placate my anger.

The cycle repeated, and repeated, and repeated. We didn't experience any kind of miracle moment whatsoever.

Mmmm, happy anniversary to us!

On one particularly stormy evening, I stood across the kitchen from Dave with a mug of steaming tea in my hands. I don't remember what we were fighting about. I do remember that the distance between us matched the distance I felt in my heart. I looked at him and felt nothing but contempt. *I've made a mistake*, I thought.

I don't know what he said next, but whatever it was, my hand began to tremble as I stared down at my tea. I felt so misunderstood, so frustrated, and so powerless, I decided the only solution was hurling my near-boiling cup of tea *right in his smug face.*

I didn't.

I walked (well, stomped) out of the kitchen. I busied myself with work. When I snuck into bed that night, I turned away from him and took great pains not to touch him. I took the distance I felt and multiplied it by ten, making sure he paid for his words with my physical and emotional coldness. I let the thought *I've made a mistake* fester in my mind and take root. It flourished like a weed in the summer sun, sprouting up quickly. For the next few months, every time I was frustrated, I retreated to the safe place in my mind where I began to dream of a life without Dave, where I could be free of the shame I felt about seemingly not being able to make our marriage work.

Turns out, I was fighting the wrong fight. The fight wasn't against Dave—it was against both of our selfish natures—the ones that want to be right, to win at all costs, to dominate the other. The reason I know that the zero-sum game doesn't work in relationships is that I tried and perfected it, and it failed miserably. But that season wasn't the end for Dave and me—it actually became a new beginning, a time of learning a new way to live and love. Looking back on that season and living with who we are now is my proof that miracle moments still happen.

Fifteen years after that season in our marriage, I wrote an article called "A Visit with the Bride." I wrote from the position of going back to my twenty-year-old self on her wedding day to prepare her for what was to come. Here's an excerpt:

> You'll make him cry in month 20 when you want to give up and get out. You'll catch a glisten in his eye under the streetlight as you drive over a bridge, and with a passion you almost never see, he'll tell you that when you said those vows, you became a team, and you can't get off that team.
> His frustration and passion and those tears will knit your heart to his, another time you'll tie the knot. . . . That bridge you crossed was an important one, because in month 20 you will move from "me" to "we."[1]

It wasn't until that moment of vulnerability that I began to believe that it could be different, for Dave and for me. And it was only through that healing and growing that I realized it could be different for all of us, if we are willing to position ourselves for miracles.

But here's the reality: Tension is not going away. (Remember, *nice is bad.*) We will always experience some stress in our relationships as we struggle to express what's inside of us and work to meet one another's needs. But the "against you" tension is a product of competing with one another, and it leads to disappointment, defensiveness, and distance.

The positioning for miracles is still a fight—but rather than the "against you" tension, this brings a "with you" tension. When it comes to aligning with others, we need to *collaborate* to win. We still struggle and strain, but now we struggle together, *with* each other. We find out what we each want and struggle *together*. Our shared enemy is now the disappointment, defensiveness, and distance that kill relationships. It's the posturing and insecurity that kill productivity in the workplace. It's the superficiality and loneliness that kill our souls. A good fight is one in which we all win.

Before we can even dig into the skills we need to activate this new way in relationships, we have to start with what we need to believe about ourselves.

Winners Know Themselves

One of my friends uses a definition of leadership he adapted from Edwin Friedman: "a self-defined individual with a non-anxious presence."[2] I think this defines those who win in relationships as well. In order to fight for the right things, a winner must become "self-defined." At first glance, you might find this disturbing. *Shouldn't I be defined by my faith, or by my family? Isn't it selfish to be "self-defined"?* But self-defined doesn't mean being selfish; it means being aware. Such people are on a progressive and courageous journey of self-discovery, becoming more attuned to their purpose and needs. Winners know *who they are* as individuals.

One of my clients recently created a list of things that he wanted to do in his life, in categories such as family, faith, travel, and physical health. He loosely based his work off Pastor Mark Batterson's Life Goal List.[3] As we reviewed the list together, I noticed he had kept several of the items from Batterson's original list on his own.

"So you want to climb Mt. Kilimanjaro?" I asked.

He paused. "Well . . . I'm not sure."

"You want to climb a mountain?"

He paused again. "Um, not really."

"OK," I replied. "Maybe we should take that one off."

We moved on. "You want to write a book?" I asked.

Another pause. "Well, I don't know."

"Do you really want to write a book?"

"I guess not."

"Hmm, OK. Let's take a minute here."

I knew my client was facing something many of us relate to: *He didn't really know who he was.* He was not self-defined. He had spent his life being others-defined. He was defined by his family, defined by his work, defined by an ideal that he had picked up and carried around for years.

When we are others-defined, conflict in relationships is even harder. When we are confronted or critiqued or challenged by others, we feel like our entire identity is on the line. After all, if I'm only living by ideals that I've perceived are important for those around me, the minute someone challenges my point of view or violates my boundaries, I experience that as a critique of my whole self. And when the self is threatened, it responds defensively (or to put it another way, is willing to throw hot tea in the face of the one who brings that feeling to the surface!).

As we continued our work together, my client revealed how pressured he felt by the examples on the life list to create "big goals" (his words). But as we continued to explore, he edited his list to include these items:

- I want my children to have a strong relationship with their grandparents.
- I want to be an attentive husband.
- I want to lead a Bible study.

What my client did was reach inside for the accomplishments that would meet *his* needs. In doing so, he became self-defined.

The second half of the definition is a "non-anxious presence." A non-anxious presence means that you are secure in yourself. You are able to receive another person's hurt or anger or frustration without feeling threatened. You are able to face your own emotions in a way that allows you to release, reassign, or respond appropriately in the moment (we'll learn how to do that in an upcoming chapter). You're able to deal appropriately with your own fears and insecurities so that you don't spew your own anxiety onto every person around you.

Imagine living into yourself with full conviction of your values and with a non-anxious presence. Imagine how you might handle your most challenging relationships if you felt neither threatened nor scared. Perhaps you have not yet connected your own emotions to the struggle at hand. Or maybe you know deeply that your others-centered orientation keeps you uncertain, insecure, and anxious about who you are and what you can become.

Either way, take heart! Remember that becoming a self-defined individual involves a progressive and courageous journey of self-discovery. Along the way you become progressively less threatened by conflict and challenging conversations, knowing that these relational challenges bring growth. Knowing who you are, what matters to you, and how to hold to those values with courage and confidence is what will allow miracle moments to happen in your life.

And although we may have different values and passions, we all have some important things in common:

We are all wired for purpose

All of us want to know our lives matter. I once heard pastor and author John Ortberg say, "As human beings, we are uniquely wired to be able to imagine a future." King Solomon, called the richest and wisest king who ever lived, said that God "has planted eternity in the human heart."[4] We have been given the gift of imagining and contributing to a future beyond ourselves, one that can leave a mark on generations to come.

Purpose, for you, might look like having a strong marriage and family. It might look like earning enough money to provide for those you love and give them a better start at life than you had. It might look like making a contribution to science, medicine, business, or education. It might look like creating beautiful things. It might look, to borrow from my client's goals, like a life of hospitality and welcome, in which others feel free to explore their faith.

Purpose means contributing to more than your own survival, but bigger doesn't mean better—unless that's part of *your* unique purpose. So whether it's being the CEO of a Fortune 100 company or growing a garden, whether it's discovering a cure for cancer or breaking the chains of generations of addiction in your own family, discovering the purpose that fulfills you is a step toward self-definition. When we know what we value, we are able to hold to those values with conviction even in the face of challenge. When we understand our purpose, we are able to weather conflict with the confidence to know it's worth it.

Many of us struggle to know our purpose, but it doesn't have to be intimidating. It can start with a simple exercise:

Imagine you get to time travel and see yourself in the future. It's your ninetieth birthday party, and the toasts are beginning. What would you want the people closest to you to say about you in those toasts?

Becoming courageous in our relationships starts with identifying what we want to see ourselves become—what characteristics and actions are most meaningful to us.

We all share universal human needs

In addition to being wired for a purpose beyond ourselves, we all share universal needs designed for our survival and flourishing. The American psychologist Abraham Maslow categorized human needs into *deficiency needs* and *growth needs*.[5] We are motivated to concentrate on a deficient need until it is met. As long as the deficiency is present, the need gets stronger. For instance, if I haven't eaten in two days, I am more interested in securing a sandwich than I am in participating in a "higher" growth need, like a nuanced salary negotiation! Of course, human beings are complicated, which means that our needs and how they are met are fluid and sometimes interchangeable. However, in general, if I am hungry (or thirsty, or feeling unsafe), I am less likely to seek a higher need, like discovering my purpose.

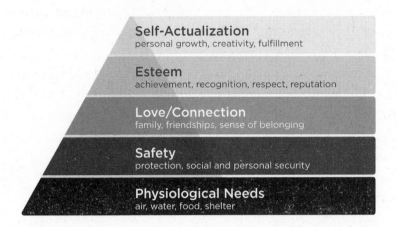

Interestingly, only the top of the pyramid—self-actualization—is considered a growth need. The rest are deficiency needs. The less we have of those things, the stronger the motivation becomes to meet those needs. Some deficiency needs are obvious: food, water, air, safety. Others, though, are less so. Did you know that love and belonging and esteem are also considered deficiency needs? As human beings, we have the need to belong—to be a part of a group. We have the need for friendship and affection, and for the ability to give and receive love. We have esteem needs as well: We need respect, mastery, dignity, independence.

Now, this may seem obvious to you and not at all helpful. After all, how is understanding a hierarchy of needs going to help you renegotiate your salary? Well, consider this: If we know how human beings work, we can better understand how to win when it comes to getting people what they want.

If I want to renegotiate my salary but just ended a long-term relationship and realize that my workplace now meets my need for belonging, I probably am not in the best position to fight for a salary increase because

I have another, more primary need that I fear won't be met if my salary conversations go south. Aha! Knowledge is power.

Many of us lack the skills needed to know our worth. We were not taught that our needs for connection, belonging, respect, and esteem are healthy and good. We may have been taught that "big boys don't cry"—stunting our growth in vulnerability and connection. We may have been told that "God helps those who help themselves"—stunting our growth in connection and belonging. But it's never too late to learn new skills. What defined you yesterday doesn't have to define you today.

So winners know who they are—their wiring for purpose and their human needs—and they also know *what they are worth*. In case you need reminding, here is what you are entitled to as a human being:

- You are entitled to seek your purpose.
- You are entitled to respectfully share your opinion.
- You are entitled to healthy boundaries.
- You are entitled to say no to being belittled, criticized, bullied, or manipulated.
- You are entitled to become healthier, more vulnerable, more open, and more loving than you used to be.
- You are entitled to grow and change.

In her book *Rising Strong*, author and psychologist Brené Brown calls this part of the journey *the rumble*. She says, "The most dangerous stories we make up are the narratives that diminish our inherent worthiness."[6] To rumble is to reckon with the truth—to deal with our inner world (self-awareness) so we can engage with our outer world, with all its love and loss and joy and pain. A winner knows this truth: Everyone's core human needs are important, including my own, *and* my life is bigger than just meeting my own personal needs.

We all have blind spots

I've often said that looking at your life and purpose is like standing with your nose against a skyscraper and trying to estimate its height. We are so close to our life that we often have an inaccurate view of it. If we're fortunate, we have a courageous friend, mentor, or teacher who can back away from the skyscraper and tell us what they see, enabling us to gain perspective.

A few years ago, I was struggling deeply with a career decision. I couldn't seem to see beyond what was right in front of me, and I felt confused and trapped. I tried hard to figure it out on my own (old patterns die hard!) but finally brought the situation to several friends and mentors. It was only when I realized that all of them unanimously (without consulting one another!) were able to see a blind spot in my leadership that was keeping me stuck that I got courageous enough to make a change.

Because we've been raised by people who also have blind spots in a world full of other people with blind spots, we develop defenses to handle all that blindness. For some of us, that looks like an arc toward pride and self-righteousness. For others, it looks like an arc toward self-pity and codependency. We are prone, with our noses against the skyscrapers of life, to have either a too high or a too low opinion of our own self-worth.

Do any of the statements in the chart on page 44 ring true for you? If so, congratulations! You've just shed light on what used to be a blind spot. If you know you are prone to be proud, or to be harsh with yourself, your growth begins with this awareness. The next few chapters will help you recognize these deficits in yourself so that you can recalibrate toward the person you want to become.

When you know you aren't the one who has it all figured out—or alternatively, when you don't assume that you are the stupid one and everyone else has the upper hand—you are allowing a new way of viewing relationships to grow in you.

Winners know who they are and what they are worth, and they are willing to work to develop the skills needed to live into that reality. And winners, by knowing what they want and what they are worth, also know what's worth working on and what they don't want or won't tolerate. This kind of knowledge is power. Knowing who we are and what we are worth gives us the power to fight for the good in our relationships. It gives us the power to pause when we want to react, to engage when we want to dismiss. When we know where we want to go, we are more likely to prepare to get there—with new ways to communicate, new ways to say yes and no, and new ways to position ourselves for the miracle moments that create a life of deeper connection, deeper understanding, and deeper meaning.

Right about now, you might be thinking that diving this deep into your purpose, your hidden needs, and your blind spots is just too much to take on. You might be thinking that with this much going on under

DEVELOPING AN ACCURATE SELF-IDENTITY

I might have a "too high" opinion of myself if:	I might have a "too low" opinion of myself if:
I am consistently frustrated by not getting "my break."	I constantly berate myself or put myself down in my inner dialogue.
I think I deserve the jobs, money, or accolades that others have who are much more educated/experienced/hardworking.	I believe I have no say in how people treat me or speak to me.
I want big wins in life, but I'm not consistent with the small integrity checks of daily life.	I want more for other people than I believe I can have for myself.
I justify my bad behavior because "he/she/they made me do it."	I justify not standing up for myself because "I made him/her/them do it."
I have a pattern of distant or broken relationships in my life.	I fear if the people in my life knew what I really need or want, they would reject me.

the surface, it's going to be too hard to do anything different, or to even believe that it's possible to change. Remember our second law of change? *Chaos before order.* We have to deconstruct before we can rebuild. Before we can win at a life we love, we have to know what we believe.

> Winners know who they are and what they are worth, and they are willing to work to develop the skills needed to live into that reality.

The first step to growth is awareness. What happens next is up to you. You can stay the same and get the exact results you are currently getting. Or you can awaken to a new reality: You don't have to keep giving away your power to a lie that's hindering your happiness and freedom. It may take some dedicated work to move into healthy and loving self-definition. It might take therapy or coaching. It might mean that things feel chaotic before they become ordered. But once you recognize a blind spot, you are at a turning point. You can commit to moving into a life where you become a self-defined, non-anxious person who is ready and willing to communicate your needs and own your blind spots, or you can stay the same. The choice is yours.

Winners Are Negotiators

During my human-behavior training as the babysitter of the rambunctious Reeds, I learned quickly that if I engaged in a battle of wills with three kids only slightly younger than me, I would most certainly lose. On my first night of babysitting, the kids managed to drink soda with dinner (not allowed), convince me there was no bedtime on the weekends (not true), and trash the house from top to bottom (allowed only in the basement). Luckily, this was the 1980s when kids ran wild and free, so apparently neither my parents nor the Reeds had any problem with an eleven-year-old babysitting until one o'clock in the morning. By that time, I had managed to tire out the kids, clean up the mess, and confiscate the soda evidence. Still, I knew that if I was going to be victorious and secure my own TV-watching and junk-food-consuming evenings away from my annoying siblings, I had to figure out how to manage these kids.

Being raised in a military family, I thought authority was non-negotiable. So when I used a win/lose scenario with the kids, also known as "My way or the highway" . . . they chose the highway. And I lost—they drank the soda, bounced off the walls, and trashed the house. I watched helplessly, cleaned up after they dropped off to sleep, and fell exhausted onto the couch just a few minutes before the parents walked through the door.

Reed kids: 1. Nicole: 0.

Most of us have been taught only the kind of negotiating I tried on the Reed kids, called positional bargaining.[7] Both parties state what they want and then defend their position in an effort to convince the other that they are right. As they argue, they become more entrenched in their corner until a battle of wills develops. The authors of *Getting to Yes* explain the process this way:

> When negotiators argue over positions, they tend to lock themselves into those positions. The more you clarify your position and defend it against attack, the more committed you become to it. The more you try to convince the other side of the impossibility of changing your opening position, the more difficult it becomes to do so.[8]

At this point, emotions come into play. Suppose you tell your teenager that she needs to clean up the bathroom after taking a shower. You argue that because she was the last one to use it, she needs to tidy the room before heading down to breakfast; your daughter argues that her little brother is the one who left his towel on the floor and toothpaste all over the counter. You defend your position, she defends hers. As the spar continues, you are likely to feel less and less understood because you believe that if your daughter were *listening*, then clearly she would *know you were right* (lies). At some point, the argument is likely to get personal. Now the fight isn't about who left the wet towels on the floor (circumstance); it's about how *disrespectful she is* (character). As your frustration increases and you each become more entrenched in your position, you will hit a breaking point. The gloves come off, and you now wield your most dangerous weapon: power.

- Power is what's used when a frustrated parent yells to a teenager, "As long as you live in this house, you abide by my rules."

- Power is what's used when two coworkers lock horns and go to their managers to complain. They have lost the negotiation and now must use power (higher authority) to get their way.

- Power is what's used when a husband and wife argue over spending habits and the breadwinning spouse ends the conversation with "because I make the money, that's why."

The "loser" in the argument now has to interpret their experience. The "loser" who gave up their position is likely to take it personally. Resentment builds. Affection is withheld. The battle might be over, but it is not forgotten. And the next time a conflict brews, the "loser" in the last exchange is already wary and wounded. Every fight becomes subsequently harder—the triggers happen faster. Moving from constructive to destructive conversation happens more quickly.

The problem with power is that when it comes to relationships, the one who has more may win the moment, but it's actually a loss. When power is deployed, the heart is lost. And when the heart is lost, the opportunity for a miracle moment is lost. Miracle moments happen when we fight for the heart, not fight for position. When one person in the relationship loses, both parties lose. You lose closeness. You lose understanding. You lose trust. Positional bargaining is a lose-lose situation. Although positional bargaining may work in the military, even military leaders know that when authority has to be deployed in order to make things happen, everyone has already lost.

At age eleven, I learned quickly that if I continued to use positional bargaining, my employment with the Reeds would be very short. The shopping spree to the Springfield Mall was not worth getting paid three dollars an hour to get my butt kicked by three little tyrants. So I had to come up with another plan. What I didn't know then was that there's a word for this kind of bargaining: win-win negotiating. Working with the Reed kids required conveying positive intent and commitment. Conveying intent was about separating the people from the problem, and focusing on our mutual interests rather than my corner of the room. It required finding creative ways we could all win: the kids, me, and the parents. Although my methods were not very sophisticated, they were just clever enough to get the kids to (mostly) comply.

I spent the next three years babysitting as my primary gig, until I entered early retirement at fourteen, when I became far more interested in hanging out with friends and talking about boys than conducting complicated negotiations over Disney movies, whose turn it was to clear the table, and whether or not *Knight Rider* was an age-appropriate TV show.

Since then, the stakes have become much higher and require more, as our early years of marriage proved. But the same principles apply. To find a mutual win, you have to make sure you are both pulling for the same side in the tug-of-war of life. Winners look for another option, knowing they are not completely right or wrong. Winners learn and practice the skills of negotiation, which we will cover in the coming chapters.

In the end, *winners hope wildly for victory but learn from defeat.*

Being a winner when it comes to relationships doesn't mean that every relationship will work out. It does mean, as one of my friends loves to say, you "fail forward." Failing forward is about owning broken and breached relationships for what they truly are—losses. When we lose something, whether that's a job, a relationship, or even trust within a relationship, we need to acknowledge the loss. Sometimes we let ourselves down and step away. Sometimes the other party lets us down and leaves us. Whether we control the leaving or the leaving happens unexpectedly to us, we feel losses deeply. We may even become scared to try again. But winners forge ahead. Wreckage from the past is a reminder that life can be painful, but it doesn't mean that there isn't good that can come from it. We can reframe painful experiences, viewing them as a chance to learn, grow, and try again—whether that's in a job, with a child, or in our next hard conversation with our mom, spouse, or best friend.

Every person I know going for a big life—a big, full, free life—has had a fall-on-your-face kind of loss. How we handle the apparent defeats we experience is far more important than how we handle the easy victories. Figuring out the Reed kids was easy; figuring out how to confront an employee, how to forgive a teenager, how to own my own brokenness—that's hard. But winners hope wildly for the victories while preparing for the possibility of defeat, because everyone will face losses at some point.

After a recent challenging season, I spent more than a year working with a spiritual director, sitting quietly and listening to what God was teaching me through a painful "defeat" experience. In one of our sessions, my spiritual director leveled with me. "You will be betrayed again," she said.

I shook my head. I knew she was right, but I just wanted it to be wrong.

"You have two choices," she went on. "You can risk love and face betrayal again, or you can betray your very self."

We can hope wildly for victory but prepare soberly for defeat. Life will hand us both. But to choose not to live into the fullness of our essential human needs is to choose to betray ourselves. This is the challenge we all face. Winning is about accepting that challenge and fighting it out for love.

〰〰〰

Questions to Consider

1. Have you ever written a life list? If so, what is on it? How does that relate to your sense of purpose and worth? If not, consider writing a list with at least five to ten things that are important to you in the areas of spirituality, relationships, vocation, and experiences/travel.

2. Reference the list on page 42 that specifies what we are all entitled to. Which ones resonate with you? Are there any statements that you are prone to not believe are true for you specifically?

3. Are you aware of any blind spots in your relationships right now? Where might you have a tendency toward inaccurate self-perception? Some common blind spots include how well we listen, our openness to different perspectives, how well we receive feedback, whether we focus on ourselves or others in conversation, and our ability to seek forgiveness.

PART ONE

MEAN WHAT YOU FEEL

If you don't lead your feelings, your feelings will lead you.

CHAPTER 4

WHY FEELINGS ARE SO HARD TO FIND

〰〰〰〰

Of all deceivers fear most yourself!
SØREN KIERKEGAARD

WHEN WAS THE LAST TIME you delayed beginning a difficult discussion—or avoided it altogether? Most of us could name a conversation *right now* that we are putting off—perhaps imagining (and hoping!) the situation will somehow resolve itself. That was certainly the case for Matt, who somehow had the patience of the Dalai Lama when it came to "waiting out" a conflict. Matt and his wife began meeting with me when Matt was unsure whether he should leave the ministry position that he'd held for several years. After months of clear and careful deliberation, the couple had committed themselves to making the change. As the final step in the process, Matt needed to have two important conversations—one with his dad; the other with his boss. It took him weeks to even set up the first meeting, and he ended up cancelling it because of a headache. He was literally making himself sick imagining the confrontation. What's more, he was unsure how to begin the discussion, get his point across without being offensive, and confidently conclude the conversation.

By the time Matt and I met after that missed meeting, he was frustrated and anxious. What's worse, he was doubting his decision to leave his position. He began to backtrack and ruminate over every previous move. Perhaps it wasn't time to leave, he told me, and maybe all this angst was a sign that he was moving too quickly. I reminded him of the process he and his wife had undertaken to make their decision and asked him, "Other than facing these conversations, is there any factor that has changed since you committed to make this move?"

He sighed heavily and put his forehead into his hands. "What is wrong with me?"

We can all relate to situations like this. We've committed to a course of action, but when we actually move toward making it happen, we balk, particularly when the stakes are high. I knew the stakes for Matt were probably even higher than he realized:

- He had expressed his insecurities over being the main provider for his family and had just found out his wife was pregnant. The stakes felt high emotionally.
- I knew from previous conversations that once the decision was made, the next step would be talking to his dad about his decision, and Matt sensed he would not approve. This step would lead to another difficult conversation. The stakes felt high strategically.
- The leader that Matt needed to talk to had been a very important part of his life when he was a teenager, and Matt feared this person would feel rejected by Matt's decision. The stakes felt high interpersonally.

As we worked through these issues, Matt relaxed a bit. "I guess I didn't really think through why this conversation was actually feeling so hard for me, but it makes sense. The stakes really are high!"

Higher Stakes, Higher Emotions

You may not resonate with Matt's story because you see yourself as someone who leads by logic when it comes to making decisions. You are a measured "thinker" whose emotions aren't in play when it comes to high-stakes relationships at love or work. Or perhaps you are a "feeler"—highly attuned to your emotions as the best guide for decisions. You lead with your heart and view your feelings as a good judge of character and guide to decision-making. Most of us lean one way or the other—but both tendencies are fraught with problems.

So are you a thinker or a feeler?[1]

Why does the way you make decisions matter? First, if we are to grow, we have to recognize that good people experience decision-making, conflicts, and relationships differently. Being more logical or more emotional is neither good nor bad. Regardless of our orientation, we all have growing to do—it's just a matter of understanding what that growth will look like because of how we are uniquely made.

Second, even if you score 25 in thinking and zero in emotions in the Thinker vs. Feeler quiz that follows, *you are using feelings to make decisions*—often without realizing it. I know, I know. You might not think you are. But whether you think you make decisions based on your thoughts or your feelings, you are still frustrated at how you are communicating (or you wouldn't be reading this book) *or* you are unable to get your spouse, teenager, boss, or employee to do what you want them to do (so you are looking for ammo to help your argument).

Let me share a third reason why it's important to connect with your emotions. Even when your brain doesn't want to acknowledge your feelings,

THINKER VS. FEELER IN DECISION-MAKING

Answer the following questions to understand how you view the role of logic and emotion in decision-making. Rate the following statements on a scale of 1 to 5, with 1 being "not like me at all" and 5 being "just like me."

Quiz	Rating
1. When I approach a decision, my first inclination is to make a list of pros and cons.	
2. I can feel tension between two people almost immediately.	
3. A person can think their way into any decision, as long as they are willing to be objective.	
4. I usually feel bad or guilty whenever I have to confront someone or someone disagrees with me.	
5. If it's not logical, it's not valid.	
6. Even when the other party tells me that they aren't emotional about a decision, I often interpret their behavior as negative or dismissive.	
7. When I'm in a conflict, the first thing I do is seek the logical explanation for the issue.	
8. Whether in love or war, thought leads the way and emotions follow.	
9. The tone in which something is said is as important as what's being said.	
10. When someone is hurt or sad, my first reaction is to support them emotionally.	

Scoring	Total
Tally your total from questions 1, 3, 5, 7, and 8. *A score of 20 or more indicates you have a strong Thinking orientation. Similar scores in both boxes indicate a balance between Thinking and Feeling.*	
Tally your total from questions 2, 4, 6, 9, and 10. *A score of 20 or more indicates you have a strong Feeling orientation. Similar scores in both boxes indicate a balance between Thinking and Feeling.*	

your body will help identify them! Hang with me and consider this: Our bodies are hard-wired to take in the environment around us. We've been given a sophisticated survival system that allows us to be aware of dangers in our environment and make complicated decisions for our good. We are constantly using our senses to see, touch, taste, smell, and hear so we can determine our next move. Think back to the last time you . . .

- smelled smoke
- heard screeching tires
- saw a big dog running directly at you (not one of those dogs that ends in "-doodle"—goldendoodle, labradoodle—but the kind of dog you see in police videos)
- felt something crawling on you

Those powerful sensations are received through your physical body and then interpreted in your brain's limbic system, which registers these sensations automatically and usually without your even being aware of it. Only *after* traveling through the limbic system (where you feel emotion) do you respond to these stimuli.

When you *think* about those sensations, what do you *feel*? Our brains are so powerful, we can recreate one of those moments as if it's actually happening right now. We can almost smell, hear, see, taste, and feel the same powerful sensations. (Have you ever had that creepy-crawly feeling after finding a bug or spider on yourself? Did I make you feel it even now? Isn't that crazy?)

The point of this whole exercise? Whether you know it or not, how you feel deeply impacts what you do. Think about that conversation you are putting off. Maybe even close your eyes for a moment and imagine it actually happening. What do you feel when you think about what you've been avoiding? Can you name that feeling? For most of us, the answer is probably no, other than a general "this doesn't feel *good*" sensation.

Now pay attention to what's happening in your body as you imagine this conversation. Are your shoulders tight? Do your cheeks feel warm? Are you clenching your jaw or fists? Do you feel a tightness in your chest or a weight in your stomach? Maybe a band squeezing your forehead?

Studies have shown that people universally correlate certain physical sensations in the body with particular emotions.[2] In other words, your physical body can help you understand your feelings and thoughts, and as we'll learn later, can also help you redirect those feelings so that you can balance thought and emotion during confrontational or difficult conversations.

MEAN WHAT YOU FEEL:
To mean what you feel, you must become aware of how your emotions impact your actions. In order to know the best and healthiest way to move forward in a conversation or conflict, you must recognize, honor, and interpret your emotions. Another term for "meaning what you feel" is self-awareness.

Now, if you are a feeler, you might be glad to hear that I've proven what you've known *all this time*. But hold on tight, because here's the problem with feelings: They aren't a reliable witness *on their own*. Feelings become powerful and helpful when they play nice with the more rational side of your brain, where decisions are made. The truth is, your thoughts and feelings are always harnessed together, whether you know it or not. Trying to use one without the other won't create the harmony you seek. If you want to be understood and respected for your thoughts but leave out your emotions, you won't experience alignment. The same is true if you want to be loved and appreciated for your feelings but leave out your thoughts. You need to be able to *mean what you feel* if you are going to be able to *say what you mean*.

Let's go back to Matt for a moment. During our many conversations about leaving his job, never once did he register anxiety or dread about the necessary conversations with his dad or boss. We talked about some emotions—fear of the unknown, sadness over leaving something he loved, hopefulness about the future—but it wasn't until the stakes were high and the decisions were "made" (or so I thought) that it became clear that there were other powerful emotions running silently in the background of Matt's soul.

These emotions deeply influenced his ability to confront these important people in his life. They were connected to previous experiences, to powerful sensations of approval, disappointment, expectations, and ultimately, Matt's own deep sense of failure or shame. Often we get clues about what our emotions might be trying to tell us. Like pieces of a puzzle, they emerge as we practice being curious, not condemning about our story. Those puzzle pieces in Matt's life had flashed briefly throughout our previous coaching sessions. Once Matt mentioned in passing that his dad often joked that "the only reason to work in ministry is if you can't do a real job." In another conversation, Matt commented on a text his mentor had sent him that morning, telling him that Matt's call to ministry was his mentor's greatest success.

Taken individually and at face value, neither of those experiences necessarily adds up to Matt's paralyzing indecision. But memories have the power to create narratives about who we are and who we must remain. We are "meaning machines," constantly interpreting new data to fit into the framework of our story.[3] And although one passive-aggressive joke and one high-expectation text might not be enough to derail Matt, if he lacks self-awareness about how those messages impact the narrative he already believes about himself, he will stay stuck. That is why the stakes feel so high and why Matt keeps avoiding these difficult conversations! We usually feel things most deeply in the relationships that matter most.

Let's project what could happen next for Matt. If he allows his feelings to drive his decision-making, he will be overwhelmed by the powerful desire to honor these authority figures and avoid shame. He will interpret his feelings to mean that he should not leave his job, which will ultimately lead to unhappiness and stress. If Matt decides to ignore his feelings and move forward with his decision, he is more likely to avoid or distance himself from these valuable relationships. He may lie or twist the truth about why he's leaving when he talks with his dad and boss, or he may end up acquiescing, shutting down, or blowing up during these conversations. This approach will also lead to unhappiness and stress.

Remember when we talked about the fight? *A violent struggle with weapons involved.* Matt is in a danger zone. If he changes his mind right now about a decision that he and his wife agreed was a good one, he's damaging his future, both in work and in love. If he plows forward with his decision before dealing with his desire to avoid shame and disappointing others, he's setting himself up for a conversation in which he isn't fully present and self-aware. This means he'll be unequipped to hold his ground with kindness and courage. If, however, Matt recognizes what's driving his fear over these conversations, then a miracle moment becomes possible. If Matt can do the work of not allowing past experiences with his dad and mentor to hold him hostage for his future decisions, he will find that it's possible to be both courageous with his life and vulnerable and open with his love and honor for both men.

Matt needs to *mean what he feels* before he can *say what he means.* And just to be clear, *"meaning what you feel" is about knowing what you feel, why you feel it, and what to do about it.* Meaning what you feel is about honoring and interpreting your feelings in order to make good decisions. It's about knowing which feelings are related to the present moment, and which feelings might be holding you in your past. It's about the conscious awareness of how your emotions influence your thoughts, and how to use them to bring about good rather than harm.

Knowing What You Feel

It seems ridiculous to think that we can't understand our own feelings, but it's quite normal to struggle to make sense of what's happening inside, particularly if you've never paid attention to how your feelings impact your actions. As we've discovered, we first experience our feelings as bodily sensations. Think of common ways of expressing emotions: skipping with joy, trembling with fear, being hot-tempered, or hanging our head in shame. If we practice being *curious, not condemning*, we may discover that we are much more comfortable with some emotional states than others.

Take a look at the feeling wheel on page 62. Working from the inside out (from basic to nuanced words), which emotions are you comfortable expressing? By the way, if you want to know what you are comfortable with, you may need to ask a self-aware and healthy family member or close friend to complete this exercise for you: (1) Circle the emotions you've seen me express. (2) Of those emotions, are there any that I seem uncomfortable talking about or acknowledging?

If you love this exercise and can't wait to talk the night away about your feelings, awesome! If your loved one agrees that you have a great grasp on what you feel and why, even better! You may not need the next few pages—but most likely there's a child, coworker, or boss you are about to understand much better if you keep reading.

On the other hand, if the feeling wheel exercise makes you want to run for the hills or roll your eyes and shut the book, I get it. The great paradox of self-awareness is that the more you resist it, the more you need it. Being vulnerable can be particularly difficult because we've all felt unsafe and unloved sometime in our past, and we still carry those experiences—particularly the ones from our childhood. Many of us have spent years, decades, or an entire lifetime avoiding the feelings we are now talking about.

The Feeling Wheel

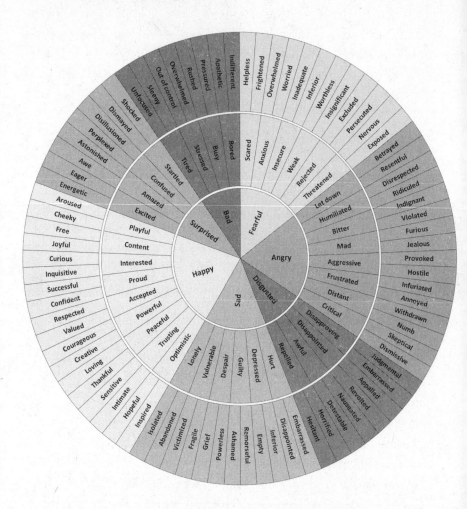

To find your feelings, start in the middle with the seven primary emotions. Then move outward to pinpoint the feeling further.
(Image courtesy of Geoffrey Roberts)

If this resonates with you, then you are proba
perhaps you have already closed yourself off and inva
(Gotcha! Stick with me—this will help you get more
without turning into a cream puff, I promise.) Let m
you don't have to participate in years of therapy or ~~~~~~~
feely" in order to find success in your relationships at home and work.
However, this is an opportunity for you to take a *small is big* step
toward understanding why in the world it seems like everyone around
you is too sensitive. This is especially true if . . .

- you've ever been told you are distant, passive, or intimidating;
- your words or actions have hurt other people and *you had no idea* until someone pointed it out;
- you've become frustrated because others seem to take everything so personally; or
- you have a pattern of relationships where people seem to betray you, leave you, or otherwise fade out of your life.

If that describes you, then most likely, you are not in touch with a
wide range of your emotions, and you come by this tendency naturally.
You may have been raised by parents who instilled in you that "boys
don't cry." You may have had to be the powerful one in order to protect
an unhealthy—or worse, addicted or abusive—parent. You may have
had painful or traumatic experiences when you needed to separate from
your emotions in order to survive—to keep yourself alive at the kitchen
table, on the playground or bus, or in the classroom. You learned how
to do your best with the situation you were in, and that was necessary
back then. Even if you have happy memories of your early years, you
may have difficulty connecting with your feelings. This isn't all about
traumatic childhoods—except for the truth that childhood is somewhat traumatic for everyone.

ıt no matter what your childhood was like, it's time to throw off ıything that isn't working for you anymore. The apostle Paul said, "When I was a child, I talked like a child, I thought like a child, I reasoned like a child. When I became a man, I put the ways of child-hood behind me" (1 Corinthians 13:11, NIV). Most of us think of this as a reason we should listen *less* to our emotions. But this sentence appears within 1 Corinthians 13, the great "love chapter" of the Bible. It's the source of the oft-quoted verses on love that you hear at wed-dings: "Love is patient. Love is kind. . . . It keeps no record of wrongs." Paul talked about becoming a man in the context of embracing a vulnerable, strong, self-sacrificing love. Becoming a man (or woman) is about putting childish ways behind us—including some powerful self-protection tools we picked up early on. Remember, meaning what you feel is about knowing *what you feel, why you feel it, and what to do about it.*

Why You Feel It (or Don't)

Emotions are tricky things. They can dictate your life. They can be acted upon rashly. They can be denied or suppressed completely. But learning to respect and respond to your emotions without letting them run the show is necessary in order to grow. To get what you need and to accomplish your purposes in life, you must learn to dance with your emotions.

Several years ago, my husband, Dave, and I were given private ball-room dancing lessons in exchange for some writing we did for the company. We do not have a good track record for dancing together, but I love it and was sure we would be gliding across the dance floor in no time. But even though we had been married more than fifteen years, learning to dance was awkward. We both needed to master new skills, not to mention the complex interchange of eye contact, hand pressure, and memory needed to stay on the beat and connected, and to move in the same direction.

In many ways, learning to dance with our emotions can feel the same way. It's awkward at first. Emotions don't make it easy for you to dance with them. They'd rather take center stage and be completely in charge, or else hide in the shadows and be ignored altogether. But the best version of you comes from a coordinated dance of your thoughts and emotions, working in rhythm to help you understand your needs and accomplish your purposes. Before you can dance, however, you have to understand what triggers your emotions, why emotions are sometimes hard to access, and how to invite them to dance.

We've already talked about how we can use our physical bodies to locate and name our emotions. By practicing *curious, not condemning*, you can become more in tune with your responses to a variety of scenarios. You'll begin to recognize how your thoughts and emotions dance with one another, not only by being aware of what's going on around you, but also by what you are physically experiencing inside of you. Depending on your current level of self-awareness, you may already be able to recognize trends in your life:

- How you think when you are happy. (For instance, you may feel more confident and relaxed or find it easier to make decisions. You are more likely to ignore red flags in relationships and less likely to be judgmental of the words and actions of others.)
- How you think when you are scared or anxious. (You might be possessive or risk averse, or you might be more likely to assume the worst.)
- How you think when you are sad. (You might be less motivated to think logically, more likely to expect defeat, and less likely to notice others.)

- How you think when you are stressed. (You might be less likely to think clearly or more likely to "blank out" or be defensive.)

Of course, we are all complicated creatures with a variety of reactions to different emotions, but if you pay attention, you'll begin to notice your tendencies when you are in a good or bad mood.

Now let's talk about a few common pitfalls of the dance between your emotions and your thoughts, particularly emotional triggers and how to reframe them.

The Truth about Triggers

Emotional triggers are like the beginning of a well-known song that you can't help but follow the moves to. Imagine yourself preparing for a lively foxtrot when all of a sudden "The Chicken Dance" blasts from the speakers. Now you find yourself flapping your elbows like wings and wiggling your backside like a duck. Not exactly the plan. You can walk into a meeting with a plan to delicately foxtrot with your thoughts and emotions, but then your boss ignores your proposal or a coworker shuts down your question, and the next thing you know, you are replaying the whole thing in your head for the rest of the day, anxious you are about to lose your job. Chicken dance.

You can be ready to waltz into a date night with your spouse, when out of the blue, he or she begins to express concerns about your oldest daughter and how she needs you to step up and be more present. You feel your frustration growing because you thought you were doing a great job with the kid and your spouse is blowing everything out of proportion. You begin to tune out the conversation, but maybe you accidentally roll your eyes, because the next thing you know, your "date" becomes a volley of insults. You drive home in silence, and each

of you hugs the edge of the bed like the other has a c
Chicken dance.

Triggers are rooted in the past

We are all susceptible to emotional triggers, times when our brains go on autopilot and we respond to situations before we are even aware of what we are doing. Our triggers tend to connect to previous good and bad experiences in our lives. Let's start with good triggers. Have you ever met someone and immediately liked and respected that person? Whether it's a customer service rep who makes you feel at ease and quickly deals with your problem, a new coworker who likes the same sports team, or a neighbor who hits the right note of friendly but not nosy, we've all had the experience of feeling immediately at ease with someone. Why is that? It's actually quite strange. You have no basis for liking this person except one brief experience, and let's face it, all people can be hard to love sometimes. The reason you have generally good vibes with some people is a trigger, most likely related to good vibes with someone else. A new coworker may remind you of your little brother. A new neighbor may make you remember a fun high school friend who always made you laugh. Your customer service rep may be efficient, like your favorite team member at work. We can be triggered by good memories, which create positive expectations for other relationships.

This works in reverse as well. You find a coworker to be opinionated and judgmental, and you intensely dislike working with that person. You become curious about your reaction and realize that you also feel pretty judged by your spouse, and you feel more trapped than you like to admit. You have a friend who's going through a hard time in her marriage, and you begin to ignore her calls and texts. You become curious about your reaction and realize she reminds you of your mom and the guilt you feel after the emotionally laden conversations where she says

ng you feeling guilty and frustrated. We

when

se outweighs a normal reaction to the
d or bad);

ecoming overly aggressive or overly
onse to the moment;

- w⟍ dread in the moment (often a feeling that
centers in t⟍ ⟍ut and may include sweaty hands or an increased
heart rate or breathing); and/or
- we feel powerless to control our actions ("They made me do it").

Our emotions are not good timekeepers. When we are triggered, we are no longer responding to the moment in front of us; we are responding to many moments behind us. When a moment triggers a powerful experience from our past, our emotions treat that moment like the present. What made us feel scared or unsafe back then will make us feel scared or unsafe in the present—even if that present moment is just a passive-aggressive email from a coworker. We have to be responsive to our triggers from the past to be able to respond in healthy ways in the present.

Before we will be open to changing our reactions to our triggers, we must embrace a universal truth: *It is not our intentions that shape who we are becoming; it is our actions.* The way you respond today is who you are becoming—it is the trajectory you are on. If you cringe because you know you are yelling like your father did or withdrawing like your mother did or dropping snide comments and gossiping at the office just like you said you never would, the reality is that those actions *are* shaping who you are becoming. But the hope of our humanity is that you can be different. The scenario that used to trigger you, making you into someone you don't like? That *very same scenario* can be the start of a miracle moment—if you will slow down and pay attention to your emotions so you don't automatically start the chicken dance but respond purposefully instead.

Responses to triggers look different

Remember Jessica, whom we met in chapter 1? At our first appointment, she told me she was on the brink of divorce but that she and her husband never fought. After our initial meeting, I looked forward to talking with them together. I hoped we could uncover what might be keeping Jessica and her husband, Greg, from being able to really communicate about how things were going between them.

I met Jessica and Greg at the door of my office. It felt like the temperature in the room went down about ten degrees when they entered, and I made a mental note that based on the ice between them, it might take a bit of time to find that spark after all. Jessica sat on the couch; Greg chose a chair. I positioned my chair so that I could see both of them and waited.

Jessica broke the silence. "Well, as you can probably tell, things are not going well." She paused and glanced over at Greg, her eyes filling with tears. "I don't know how things got so bad between us. We barely talk, and when we do, it's about the kids' schedules or a bill that needs to be paid or what we need from the grocery store. I feel . . ." At this, Jessica's tears began in earnest, and she dropped her head and reached for a tissue from the coffee table in front of her. She glanced over at Greg and then back to me.

"I feel like I've tried every way I can to work things out between us, but I wonder if Greg even wants to keep trying and if he . . . loves me anymore." Jessica kept her teary gaze fixed firmly on me.

I nodded and looked at Greg, who was sitting back in his chair with his hands clasped in front of him, fingers interlaced. He looked back at me and then over at Jessica with a somewhat bewildered look on his face. He squeezed his fingers together slightly and shrugged his shoulders. I prompted him, "Greg, is there something you'd like to add to what Jessica has shared?"

Greg sighed and rubbed his head. Shrugging again, he said, "I don't know. I just don't think it's that bad."

Uh-oh.

With eyes bulging and mouth open, Jessica sat very still—the kind of still when all the waves are sucked out to sea just before a tsunami hits. She exhaled sharply, a half laugh, half bark. Looking over at Greg with an expression of unveiled disdain, she shook her head and rolled her eyes. "You have *got* to be kidding me. Unbelievable." And with that, she crossed her arms. I could practically feel the arctic winds blowing. The tears and vulnerability of the previous ninety seconds had been replaced with what I could only interpret as pure contempt.

Let's stop the scene for a moment, shall we?

Before we take sides with Greg or Jessica, let's pan out a little bit and take a look at what's happening. First, Greg and Jessica are now in a high-stakes interaction. I've been counseling and pastoring long enough to know that it's not easy to sign up for marriage counseling for the first time. Most people don't relish the idea of putting their relationship under a microscope and having their most intimate secrets and faults exposed in front of a total stranger—especially a pastor. Second, it's easy to listen to this conversation and think that only Jessica is being triggered. She is the one who's sharing vulnerable information and is overcome by tears. Jessica is the one who expresses a wide range of emotions during this interaction. But—surprise!—Greg is also being triggered.

Me, triggered? But I don't feel anything

When we are triggered, emotional eruptions can go one of two ways. We can explode (like Jessica) or implode (like Greg). Psychologists call these types of reactions to powerful emotions *defense mechanisms*. Remember how we said a fight is a *violent struggle with weapons involved*? Our defensive reactions are just as powerful as our offensive weapons. When we implode like Greg did, here are a few defense mechanisms we might use:

Dissociation. When you dissociate from your feelings, you lack the ability to connect them to the moment you are in. You've probably experienced a kind of dissociation when you've driven a familiar route and "zoned out"—you are present in body, but your mind is somewhere else. Dissociation happens on a spectrum, but when it comes to powerful emotions, dissociation is a defense mechanism we tend to use as children in situations where we feel helpless. It allows us to "leave" the threatening situation and be somewhere else. If you've seen a child hiding their face when a parent raises their voice or during a storm, you've witnessed dissociation, which in some ways is an inward experience of hiding, a way to escape a situation that feels threatening.

What's weird about dissociation is that it can often be an unconscious reaction. The person who dissociates may do it without even realizing they are doing it. For the sake of this example, let's assume we know Greg's backstory. Greg's parents divorced when he was ten. He has strong memories of feeling helpless as his mother cried. His only way to cope with that threatening experience of his mother's vulnerability and his helplessness was to dissociate from the moment. Now, as an adult, when Jessica begins to cry, he is triggered and his body shuts down. Without even knowing it, Greg's body language says that he is not present—his face is blank and he leans away from Jessica when she begins to be vulnerable. The very mechanism that used to protect Greg when his parents fought is now working against him.

Suppression or Repression. Another way our emotions can be disguised is through suppression or repression. Both reactions involve pushing unwanted emotions away. In suppression, for example, we know we are feeling sad but we "swallow it" and ignore it. In repression, we don't even allow the emotion to come into our awareness. Rather than feeling a powerful emotion—be it anger, guilt, shame, or sadness—we feel just vaguely empty. The problem with this approach is that the emotions aren't actually gone—they still reside within us and will find an outlet at some point. Rather than learning healthy ways to express emotion, many of us picked up early on that the emotion itself was not appropriate or allowed. That which is not expressed in healthy ways becomes even more powerful in the dark. Because we never learned what to do with these emotions, they feel even more dangerous and potent. Attending to the work of controlling all those triggers—and not having the words to express the emotion in the first place—may be why Greg's reaction appeared so subdued.

Projection. A third common defense mechanism involves "acting out" a buried feeling in another way. This is the "I'm not the problem; you're the problem" approach. This may look like a teen shouting, "Stop yelling at me!" when he is arguing with (shouting at) his dad.

When projecting, we take our powerful emotion and pretend it's the other person's emotion. Without knowing it, we may begin to try working out our problems by making them someone else's issue and by using criticism, sarcasm, passive-aggressive comments, or outright anger to cope with what feels impossible to deal with internally. This can happen largely outside of our awareness, but one of the ways we can bring it into the light is by asking ourselves, *Is the thing I'm annoyed by/angry at/frustrated with in this person something that also exists in me?* Using our *curious, not condemning* lens, we may, for the first time, get in touch with the vulnerable part of ourselves that's using defensiveness to cover up our vulnerability, insecurity, or pride.

This walkabout through Psychology 101 is not going to solve Greg and Jessica's problem immediately. But there can be great relief in understanding that we are struggling with one another for a reason. Greg is not an emotionless robot and Jessica is not a dramatic diva. The problem is not that "they were never right for each other," as many troubled couples begin to believe.

Sometimes all it takes is a little awareness, but most of the time, miracle moments come over time, after we've grown in self-knowledge. It doesn't happen perfectly. Remember how Matt was struggling to navigate a career decision? Over a few weeks, we worked on self-awareness and being able to release and reassign emotions that didn't belong in the conversation with his boss. Matt was ready. But he kept putting it off. And putting it off . . .

Matt and his wife wavered in their decision several times but finally agreed to move forward with the career change—and although Matt did eventually tell his boss, he just sent an email explaining that he was leaving his job for family and financial reasons. Matt had the conversation but he never really *had* the conversation. It was too awkward and scary to talk openly about his real reasons for leaving. He wanted to do the right thing and felt committed to doing it. But when the time came, he couldn't bring himself to engage. As Matt withdrew, his boss seemed to sense the distance, and after one or two half-hearted emails of congratulations, he stopped following up. Eventually, the incredibly important relationship Matt had with his boss and mentor became a fading memory. Miracle moments don't always happen, and we aren't always ready for what it takes to have the tough conversations. But I have hope for Matt—for his next decision and next difficult conversation.

Whether we need to have that tough conversation with a family member or our boss, we will communicate imperfectly. Since we were all raised by flawed parents and sustained at least the normal emotional bumps and bruises of childhood, not one human being will have an ideal relationship with anyone else—be it a spouse, a coworker, or a best friend.

My counseling mentor used to say, "A marriage is not broken.

The two people in the marriage are both broken. The healthier they become, the healthier the marriage will be." I believe the same holds true for all of our relationships, and healthy friendships and partnerships begin with self-awareness. After all, if we don't know what we feel, why we feel it, and what to do about it, how can we possibly express ourselves in a constructive way to those who *want* to know us, work with us, and be loved by us?

Remember that miracle moments happen when you have alignment—when your emotions, thoughts, and actions are integrated, allowing you to stop in the midst of a difficult conversation and commit to a new way forward. The miracle moment isn't primarily about a different reaction in the other person; it's about a different reaction in you.

∿∿∿∿∿

Questions to Consider

1. After completing the thinker/feeler assessment on page 56, would you describe yourself as more of a thinker or more of a feeler? How has that played out in your life in positive or negative ways?

2. Do you have any "chicken dance" relationships in your life? Do you find that you are more likely to be triggered by certain personality types or situations? How has that impacted your relationships overall?

3. Do you relate more with Greg's or Jessica's way of handling conflict? Do you resonate with any of the "imploding" triggers of dissociation, repression/suppression, or projection? Are there certain circumstances or relationships in which you are more likely to default to silence or withdrawal, as Matt did?

CHAPTER 5

TRUE YOU: HOW TO BECOME MORE SELF-AWARE

∧∧∧∧∧

*It takes considerable knowledge just to realize
the extent of your own ignorance.*

THOMAS SOWELL

IF YOU'VE HAD ENOUGH of the navel-gazing, I have some good news. Self-awareness is not a goal unto itself. We are not peering inward to the depths of our emotions just to drown in the deep end of everything we've ever felt and experienced. Instead, self-awareness is the first step toward getting more of what we really need in life. Our alignment comes from *meaning what we feel* before *saying what we mean*. To "mean what we feel" is to be able to accurately interpret our emotions—acknowledging the reactions, evaluating whether they are relevant to the situation or relationship in front of us, and then honoring or releasing them.

If we don't express our emotions accurately, they will express themselves for us. They may come out in a guarded posture, a passive-aggressive comment, or stonewalling—controlling the relationship by clamming up or refusing to engage. Each of these is an *emotional* reaction, even if the response is stony, silent, or blank. Naming and then responding to or releasing our emotions allows us to be present to the person we are with and ultimately to express ourselves so that others can hear us. It doesn't mean we will always get what we want, but it does mean that we open the door to meaningful conversation and clear decision-making. Self-knowledge is the prerequisite to miracle moments.

Because we are infinitely complex, however, it is not easy to measure our self-awareness. Earlier we read Paul's admonition to leave childish ways behind, which is followed by this phrase: "Now we see in a mirror dimly" (1 Corinthians 13:12, ESV). The attempt to find the truth of your soul is like getting a passing glance of your reflection as you walk by a storefront and being curious about it. Likewise, if you take in a few brief glimpses of who you are inside, your emotional world will begin to take shape. You will begin to notice patterns—some that you want to honor, and some that you are ready to let go of. The great adventure of self-awareness is getting to know yourself, and in doing so, growing in your ability to express a range of emotions.

> If we don't express our emotions accurately, they will express themselves for us.

My family is wildly intense and competitive. When the kids were little, most games ended with yelling, crying, or both. As we've all matured (especially Dave and I!), we've learned that knowing the rules of engagement makes the game itself go much better. When it comes to self-awareness, we are preparing to engage with patterns of unconscious behavior that have been in place for years. We are poking the bear of our childhood hurts. That bear might have been hibernating for a long time, or it might be hungry or ready to rage. We don't know what's there until we jab it. To pile on the analogies, we are turning over big rocks and finding out there are a lot of bugs and some dirt underneath—things we might not want to see in ourselves and certainly don't know how to change. And because we have strong emotional patterns in place, our defense mechanisms can easily be activated too—whether it's the big red button that says EXPLODE ("He/she/they made me do it"), the big red button that says IMPLODE ("I'm fine; emotions aren't a big deal"), or everyone's favorite button, DEFLECT ("*You* should read this because you are obviously the one with the problem").

The first thing to know is that no one is asking you to change right now. You don't have to lay down your weapons—yet. This exercise in self-awareness is merely about learning more about yourself and the way your emotions express themselves to the people around you. This will help you get more of what you want and less of what you don't. Agreeing to the rules of engagement prevents you from pressing the panic buttons whenever you have an uncomfortable interchange.

To start this exercise, I want you to bring to mind a challenging relationship in your life. We all have them. It's that person who's hurt you, or confused you, or who you just don't seem to understand. It might be someone from your past who you are no longer in contact with or someone with whom you interact every day. If you've had frustrating experiences with that person, you can probably bring back one of those moments with crystal clarity.

If you can't remember a particular instance, imagine yourself coming into a darkened theater. You sit down in a plush velvet seat, the curtains open, and the movie begins. Play out the movie of a moment in this relationship. Are you on the phone with this person? In your office? At home in bed before going to sleep? In the kitchen? Imagine what you are wearing and what the other person is wearing. Think about his or her posture, tone of voice, and the circumstances of the conversation.

How do you feel now? Is your stomach tightening? Is your jaw clenched? Are you feeling your defenses come up as you simply imagine this moment? OK, now that I have you sufficiently agitated, let's consider the new rules of engagement that can help you *mean what you feel*. As a starting point for this exercise, I'll give you an agitating example from my own life. (Opportunities for growth abound around here!)

As I wrote this chapter, we were under shelter-in-place orders during the Covid-19 pandemic. My children were doing school from home; my husband had taken over our home office for his work; and this book still needed to be written. I woke up early one morning to get to this chapter. Forty-five minutes into the writing, I got up from my desk to refill my coffee cup. Just then, my husband popped out from behind the corner. I used to think I was a morning person until I met my husband. When Dave gets up each day, it's as if his body is possessed by Tigger, the boundless, energetic tiger from Winnie-the-Pooh. The rest of the family looks on him with suspicion and just a touch of dread as his endless morning sunshine glares on the rest of our sleepy heads. Back to the point. So Tigger—ahem, Dave—came bopping around the corner ready to chat about how to get the kids to make their beds, what the *Today* show had said about the coronavirus that morning, and when we could take a walk that afternoon.

As I stood at the coffeepot, a strong wave of frustration rolled over me, and I responded with a cool "We'll see." Dave's face clouded over with hurt for a moment, and then he responded with a bit of grit in his voice: "Why are you being so rude to me?"

[End scene.]

Now let's pause and reflect on what's happening beneath the surface of this jab-hook marital spar:

When I said, "We'll see," I thought my reaction was 100 percent right. One. Hundred. Percent. I had no idea what I was feeling at the moment, other than annoyed. I lashed out at what was irritating me, and at that moment, that verbal slap was the rebuff to my husband who had actually been quite kind to me. *We can sometimes tell when we've overreacted to the moment we are in by the response of the other person.*

In this moment, we have a choice to make. I knew by the way Tigger's tail slumped—er, Dave turned away—that I had hurt him. I knew he thought I was rude because he told me so! Yet in the moment that I responded to him, I felt it had been perfectly appropriate. So here we approach our very first rule of engagement: In order to make any progress in self-awareness, we must willfully decide that *we are not as right as we think we are, even when we feel right.*

In the first moment of reaction, we *always* think we are completely right. We justify ourselves and our response. The problem is always someone else, not us. The first step in growth is deciding that we are not always completely, 100 percent accurate in our read on a situation. And that morning at the coffeepot, I knew that was true of me.

RULE OF ENGAGEMENT #1:

I am not as right as I think I am.

After my chilly response to Dave, which probably felt more like an aggressive "shut up," he walked away and shut the office door. I turned back to the coffeepot with my shoulders slumped, feeling a new wave of emotion—guilt for messing up a perfectly kind invitation for a walk at lunchtime. My shoulders sagged again under the weight of my own hypocrisy as I had posted a perky "look at us working from home together!" picture on Instagram just the day before. I briefly considered assuaging my guilt with a post update: "Please do not be mad at me for making it appear that all is well at home. Turns out, I am quite annoyed. I just snapped at my husband and now we aren't talking."

I had reached the moment when many of us—myself included—shut down under the weight of the shame of a failed encounter. This was the moment when I could have suppressed all that emotion and just let the interaction pass. After all, Dave was married to me—not to mention we were quarantined at home together—so he'd just have to get over it. And the truth is, knowing Dave, he would have gotten over it. But that doesn't mean I would. All the little cutting moments that pass between spouses, between coworkers, between siblings and parents and children, are constantly instructing us. And the moments when we miss one another—when we are misaligned, when we miscommunicate, when we misconstrue—all add up to less fulfilling relationships at best and, at worst, relationships that fracture and never mend. So, yes, it was just a passing comment at the coffeepot—but it was a chance for much more.

Stopping to acknowledge that we have our own blind spots in interactions even when we feel completely right is the first step of growth. However, developing our self-awareness doesn't mean we completely dismiss our reactions either.

In one hand I hold the first rule: *I am not as right as I think I am.* But in the other hand, I hold the second rule: *I am not as wrong as I think I am.*

Knowing that my reaction also has validity allows me to employ a powerful tool for self-awareness: rewinding the game tape. When we rewind the tape, we replay a moment of engagement and process what we were feeling and thinking as the moment played out. We sit down in the theater and watch the moment, replaying it a few times, until we get an accurate read on the situation. We hold out the fact that we are not completely right and we are not entirely wrong, and we find the middle ground of the situation.

RULE OF ENGAGEMENT #2:

I am not as wrong as I think I am.

That morning, my defense mechanisms kicked in strong, swinging wildly from *You, Nicole, are completely right and you should hold your ground* to *You are completely wrong and a terrible person.* When we are triggered, we have a prime opportunity to pay attention and become more aware of our inner, emotional world. But in order to understand ourselves, we must lay down our defenses.

So I took a few deep breaths and repeated *curious, not condemning* to myself. Then I replayed the game tape a few times to ask myself what I was feeling and thinking before, during, and after my interaction with Dave. I paid attention to how I was feeling and where I was feeling it in my body. It took about five minutes for me to come to an accurate sense of my emotions. (And by the way, that was after years of therapy, coaching, and spiritual direction. Training in self-awareness takes time and practice, and for me, intentional self-coaching was required to understand even a spat at the coffeepot!)

Because I know it's hard for me to name my emotions, I had to replay the moment a few times. In doing so, I realized that Dave approached me like he does on any normal morning—except this time, I was deep in my head mentally writing this chapter. I was frustrated at how hard it was to find alone time (any alone time) during a global pandemic and then feeling guilty about my mild resentment that my family was even in my writing office, aka the entire house, at 9:25 a.m. on a Tuesday. I realized that although I had been telling Dave that I fully supported him working full-time at home without interruption, underneath the surface I was frustrated and resentful that he got to focus on his work all day while I was constantly interrupted by my children. And I felt bad for thinking that way because my kids were handling the pandemic like heroes, demanding very little. Even so, the small amount they required was making me angry, irritated, and anxious. I also knew myself well enough to know that I was worried and fearful about the future, about what this huge, dark, unknown cloud of Covid-19 might mean, and about my fears that this book might not even be relevant by the time of publication.

A ten-second interaction at the coffeepot allowed me to get more honest with myself about how things really were—so that I could handle my own stuff without spewing it over everyone else. In order to *mean what we feel*, we have to accurately identify, honor, and release emotion when needed.

I walked to the office and gave Dave a real apology (more on that in

COUNT TO NINETY

You don't have to feel shut down or out of control when it comes to difficult emotional reactions. According to Dr. Jill Bolte Taylor, a neuroscientist, your body responds to an emotional moment with a ninety-second chemical process. In other words, your physical reaction—whether you feel that tightening in your gut or that "I'm gonna explode" feeling or that wash of panic or dread—will last for only ninety seconds. If you can stay present and let that minute and a half pass, you can allow your emotions to inform the moment you are in, without hitting the panic button to *explode* or *implode*.

chapter 6). Over the next few days, that moment of insight led me to talk with Dave about the support I needed, which he was happy to provide. Rewinding the game tape—at least three times—gave me the perspective I needed to interpret my emotions, honor my deeper need (to honestly express my fears and frustrations to Dave), make things right with him by apologizing for what was unhelpful (snapping at my husband who was being perfectly reasonable at the coffeepot), and release myself from any lingering guilt or shame.

Now it's your turn. Remember the frustrating or unreconciled relationship you brought to mind earlier? Take a few minutes to replay the game tape of that interaction. If you can't think of anything right now, put the book down and go live your life for an hour or two. I bet that's all the time you'll need to gather the emotions and frustrations for this experiment. This doesn't have to be a big deal—in fact, it's not helpful to start with your deepest and most broken relationship. Just your everyday, run-of-the-mill conflict is a great place to begin.

First, replay the incident in as much detail as possible. As you do, take the following steps:

1. **Pay attention to your triggers.** When exactly did you shut down or snap? What had the person just said? Did that remind you of anything else? What were you thinking about right before this interchange? Did you have any built-up frustration with this person before this moment? Are you sensing a pattern in this relationship that you don't like?

2. **Test your emotions.** As you rewind the game tape, consider what you were feeling. If your immediate emotion was anger, stay with that for a moment and consider whether there was more than just anger there. Many times, we use anger as a defense against feeling betrayed, embarrassed, vulnerable, abandoned, lonely, or helpless. Is there a deeper emotion at play that this interchange brings up?

   Remember, it doesn't matter if the situation doesn't *warrant* that kind of emotion. Practice *curious, not condemning* with yourself in order to honor what you are feeling and then place it appropriately. If it belongs with an unreconciled relationship or unhealed hurt from your past, you need to know that. Shaming yourself for feeling something deeply— even if that feeling was triggered by an interaction with your twelve-year-old—will only exacerbate the problem. When you honor the emotion by recognizing it for where it belongs, you can begin to release it when it shows up in unwanted places.

3. **Commit to who you want to be.** This is the most important part of the exercise. As long as you hold on to the idea that your reactions are justified, that he/she/they "made" you do it, that you "can't" express your emotions, etc., you have decided that you can't, won't, or don't want to change (more about that

later). And as long as that's the case, you'll have a 100 percent success rate at staying exactly the same.

In order to grow, you have to commit to who you want to be. Make this into a statement of belief that you repeat to yourself:

I want to be a person who apologizes sincerely.

I want to be a person who is even-tempered.

I want to express myself civilly and clearly.

I want to be a person who speaks up for what I need.

I want to be a person who can accept feedback.

If you have a hard time thinking of who you want to be, it may help to think of someone you admire: What qualities do they have that you want to emulate? How would you describe their presence and how that is connected to the way they interact with people? On the other hand, you might find it easier to think about who you *don't* want to be: What characteristics do they have that you want to avoid? What positive things would need to grow in you so that you don't become more of what they are? How would you describe that person's presence and the way they treat people? What positive things need to grow in you so that you treat people differently?

Reframe the positive traits into a commitment of who you want to become.

4. **Play the opposite game.** As you rewind the game tape, imagine yourself reacting in the opposite way. If you tend to stonewall or shut down, imagine yourself speaking up. If you

tend to snap or yell, imagine yourself being quiet or asking a question instead of making a statement or criticism. As you imagine the opposite reaction, your ego will most likely jump up, defensively offering all kinds of reasons why that won't work.

I've tried that before and she's just going to yell more if I speak up for myself.

No one will respect me if I don't raise my voice.

Your ego is trying to defend you by convincing you that something different will never work. That's why we aren't going to alter anything right now—we are just rewinding the game tape and listening and learning.

In order to change, we have to ask ourselves if we are willing to step out in faith and actually do something different. Remember, *small is big* in the rules of miracles. You can choose to do the opposite of what you'd normally do in one interaction at the coffeepot—it doesn't have to start with you trying to repair the thirty-year dysfunctional relationship with your mother. It can mean smiling and engaging your coworker instead of turning away and rolling your eyes. It can be responding to your teenager with a question instead of snapping off a sarcastic retort.

We play the opposite game to become more aware of those all-or-nothing statements that our egos like to make to justify our current behavior. The question is, are those statements really true? All of the time? Or is it possible that if you started responding differently, life could actually be different?

5. **Look for patterns.** Our final step in this self-awareness journey is to look for patterns. When our reaction takes us out of

the present, it's usually because of experiences from the past or worries about the future. As we rewind the game tape, we may discover a pattern with a person that needs to be addressed. Resentment from continued "misses" in the relationship can lead us to harbor anger and unforgiveness—which covers the places where we've felt vulnerable and hurt. Or we might discover that a pattern from another relationship is the one that needs to be addressed—our irritating employee isn't the problem; it's our relationship with our abrasive sister that's creating the dynamic.

Our reaction in the present can also project us into the future. Our boss tells us that we need to reduce our budget by 10 percent, and our fears for the future create a defensive response in the present. Our twelve-year-old lies about his phone use, and our fear of where this *could* go makes us react with all the force of our parenting muscle. The journey of self-awareness is about understanding when our present reaction is actually about the past or the future. We can deal appropriately with the present only when we keep our past and future in their proper places.

Patterns to Look For: Can't/Won't/Don't Want To

When it comes to our triggers, there are some universal stories that are easy to fall for—we all tend to get duped into believing these at one point or another. The authors of *Crucial Conversations* call these patterns *helpless*, *villain*, and *victim* stories[1]—which fall neatly into our categories of can't/won't/don't want to. When our ego tells us "I can't," we are believing the helpless narrative, which tells us we are powerless to change our situation. The reality is, unless we are being held forcibly against our will, we are not defenseless.

Whenever you find yourself following an "I can't . . ." trail, make

MEAN WHAT YOU FEEL

Paying attention to who you are allows you to commit to who you want to be. You will not become who you want to be without making the courageous journey into discovering the truth: What you are feeling is creating the behaviors that are giving you the results you are getting.

Miracle moments begin when you *mean what you feel*. Don't move on in this book without processing a current frustration or misunderstanding.

Bring that recent frustrating interaction to mind and then revisit it through this lens:

1. Rewind the game tape
Replay the circumstance. What triggered you? What was behind it? What did it remind you of? How were you feeling?

2. Commit to who you want to be
In thinking about that interaction, what kind of person do you want to become the next time you are in a similar circumstance? More patient? More joyful? More courageous?

3. Play the opposite game
Imagine yourself in that same scenario, having a reaction more in line with who you want to be. If you've shut down, blown up, or withdrawn, imagine yourself doing the opposite. What if you leaned in instead? What words would you say? How would you express how the moment feels?

If finding your feelings is tough for you, use the feeling wheel on page 92 to track your feelings and chart your progress.

sure you listen to what your ego is saying and then determine whether it's *really* true. Miracle moments occur when we fiercely eliminate "I can't" from our vocabulary as much as possible and replace it with the reality of choice. Just knowing you have a choice can bring great clarity about the way you are living.

I once had a client, Kendall, who was secretly in love with her childhood best friend, Andrew. When I met Kendall, Andrew had just moved to Europe without ever showing signs that he was interested in her. Kendall was frustrated and felt helpless. On the one hand, she valued her friendship too much to jeopardize it. On the other hand, she worried that she was waiting for nothing and life would pass her by while she watched Andrew walk down the aisle with some European model he met along the way, leaving her holding her unrequited love in her heart and crying into her pillow like an actress in a bad rom-com. (Can you hear the Adele song "Hello" playing in the background?)

I wanted to help Kendall reframe her experiences as a forced choice—creating a scenario with just two options to pick from. "You can choose to wait on Andrew, or you can choose to share your feelings with him," I told her.

It wasn't easy, but Kendall decided to wait. I did not have high hopes, but thankfully I was completely wrong. When Andrew came back from Europe a year later, Kendall declared her feelings with much consternation, and a year later, they were married. Miracle moment! I firmly believe that because Kendall took her power back and *decided to make the choice to wait*, she was in a position to be courageous and open when the time finally came to share her feelings.

Forced choices allow us to face the reality we are in, no matter how difficult. "Either I can choose to be belittled by my boss, or I can choose to speak up about how his actions are making me feel." "Either I can choose to walk away when I'm feeling ignored by my husband, or I can speak up

HOW TO MEAN WHAT YOU FEEL IN TWO MINUTES OR LESS

Begin by acknowledging that your emotions impact your actions. Then work to bring your emotions into your awareness by replaying the game tape and naming the feeling (or feelings) at play.

Once you can name what you feel, you can *mean* what you feel by choosing to do one of the following:

1. **Release:** If the emotion is not warranted for the situation you are in, you can name it and release it.

> Example: "I am feeling angry because I am frustrated with my preschooler for spilling the juice again when I am already late for work. I honor that I feel angry, but I am releasing it because this was an accident, and my preschooler needs my support, not my frustration."

2. **Reassign:** If the moment you are in reminds you of a past hurt or future fear, reassign the emotion to its proper place.

> Example: "I feel panicked because my boss called me into an unscheduled one-on-one meeting. I feel fearful and insecure that I have failed or messed up in some way. I honor those feelings, but realize that the level of emotion that I feel is not related to this moment but to other times in my life where I've felt fearful. I am reassigning my fear and choosing to be peaceful and present with this moment in front of me."

3. **Respond:** If the emotion honors what you need from the situation, allow it to move you to *saying what you mean*.

> Example: "I've felt distant from my spouse these last few days. Every time we interact, I find myself pulling away. As I pay attention to that response, I realize that I feel hurt because he hasn't picked up on how stressed I am about a work situation and isn't paying attention to my needs. I want to respond to this emotion and engage."

and let him know how I feel." Forced choices also eliminate the helpless narrative. Being belittled by your boss or ignored by your husband is now a choice you made, rather than a reality you were forced into. Helplessness is a choice, and the first step of self-awareness is realizing that.

The "I can't" narrative is closely linked to the victim story, which leads us to believe we are completely innocent, whether we are behaving poorly or not. This is what's in play when we believe he/she/they "made" me do it. When we are living in the victim narrative, we "speak of nothing but [our] noble motives."[2] When we paint ourselves as victims, we leave out important details about things we did or didn't say, did or didn't do, or how we acted or didn't act in the situation. Our inner dialogue says things like *I was just trying to help* or *I was just being nice.* We act bewildered and hurt by the other person without paying attention to our own behavior. We shift blame off ourselves and onto the villain—the other person in the arrangement. This is the "I won't because" narrative. "I won't change because . . ." that person is always "a jerk" . . . that person is always "an idiot" . . . that person is always "terrible" . . . that person "never listens." Look for absolutes in your inner story, words like *always* and *never* and the four-letter word of victims, *I was just . . .*

The problem with viewing dynamics through the villain or victim lens is that we stop acting like people are humans and start acting like they are cartoon characters, ourselves included. We categorize interactions and people as good or bad, wrong or right, black or white because that feels easier than dealing with the gray. If we can justify our behavior, we don't have to acknowledge our own failing and sin. If we can blame someone else, we don't have to deal with feeling vulnerable, helpless, or needy. If we can make ourselves helpless, we won't have to try—and risk failure.

Unless we see clearly through our "I can't" and "I won't" stories, we won't deal with the next obstacle in our growth: "I don't want to." If we can get to this level of honesty with ourselves, we can actually grow. Acknowledging "I don't want to" is another way of admitting *I want to keep my ego the way it is. I want to keep my story the way I'm believing it.* Dealing with "I don't want to" makes us face the truth: *I don't value this job as much as I've been saying I do. I don't actually want to work this hard on this relationship. I don't need to change; we can just stay like this. I don't want to because I'm scared this will end our relationship.*

The great thing about "I don't want to" is that it's honest. You're faced with a problem of motivation rather than a problem of fabrication. The helpless/villain/victim stories are fabrications—they are like movies "based on a true story" rather than the actual true story. When we move through those and realize that we still don't want to change, we can deal honestly with what is behind our "I don't want to"—and decide whether refusing to change is making us the person we want to become.

~~~~~~

Questions to Consider

1. Are you likely to think of yourself as more right than you are or more wrong than you are? Does that change based on the relationships you are in? If so, how?

2. One way to grow in handling your emotions in healthy ways is to complete the Chart Your Feelings exercise on pages 92–93. Another way is to "commit to who you want to be." What are one to three statements of character that describe the person you want to become?

3. In what situations and relationships are you most likely to fall prey to the "I can't" narrative? How might you reframe that frustrating situation into a forced choice?

CHART YOUR FEELINGS

For seven days, use this page and wheel to put a check mark on the feelings you experience each day. Try to find at least five emotions to name and recognize throughout your day, and identify the circumstances that led to those feelings. Start in the middle with the seven primary emotions. Then move outward to pinpoint the feeling further.

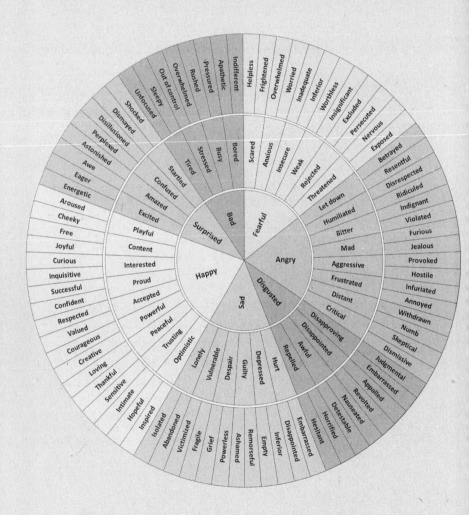

At the end of one week, look back over the feelings you checked. Record each feeling you checked and fill in the second and third columns:

Name of feeling	When did I experience this?	Did I express this feeling? How?

Choose one positive and one negative feeling from the week to process using release/reassign/respond.

PART TWO

SAY WHAT
YOU MEAN

Learn the art of
tough conversations
in three steps.

CHAPTER 6

SEEK TO UNDERSTAND

∧∧∧∧∧

The end of a matter is better than its beginning,
and patience is better than pride.
ECCLESIASTES 7:8, NIV

AS WE MOVE INTO THE REAL PRACTICE of confronting, growing through, and healing from a conflict, let's return to the story of Jessica, whom we first met in chapter 1. She came to meet with me on the verge of divorce after feeling lonely and hurt for months—maybe years. She knew what she wanted out of the relationship but had exhausted all of her methods for explaining it to her husband. She had named what he was doing wrong and told him how he needed to change. But when I asked her what she thought her husband needed from her (beyond her letting up and not being critical), she had a harder time answering.

When someone has hurt us, disappointed us, or frustrated us, we tend to know what we want out of the situation pretty quickly. Jessica's response to her husband had been to name what he was doing wrong and dictate how he needed to change it. We all come by this naturally. Surely if we're right about something, all we need to do is explain, convince, persuade, or defend our reasoning to the other person. And since we're convinced we're right, our usual response in a confrontation is to retaliate immediately once the other person begins sharing their side of the conflict. Rather than seeking to understand, we seek ammo. We begin to "fix" the other person before we even understand how they are experiencing the moment.

Now let me ask you: When's the last time that worked for you? When's the last time it worked *on* you? Most of us don't have an information problem when it comes to the choices we are making. In fact, most of us feel justified and right about the way we feel, the way we view the world, and the reasons we do the things we do, and it seems clear to us what would resolve the conflict. But learning about ourselves and others isn't like learning to cook. If I'm teaching you to bake a cake and tell you to crack the egg before mixing it into the batter, you have to crack the egg. If you mix the egg, shell and all, into the batter, you aren't going to get the same results. When the cake comes out of the oven, we'll know who's right. Yet interpreting an experience, particularly when we feel misunderstood or butt heads with someone, is not as easy as following a simple recipe. One of us wants to crack the egg in the batter; one of us wants to throw the dang egg against the wall. But if we are willing to slow down, seek understanding, and try again, we can draw on some helpful principles along the way. These principles are general guidelines that, over time, will create space for miracle moments. They are the ingredients we need to begin to create opportunities for more love, more forgiveness, and more trust in our most important relationships.

Three Steps to Move toward Understanding

Assume positive intent

The first principle is this: *If we want to fight well, the first step is to clarify and convey our positive intent.*

The word *intent* has several meanings. The primary definition concerns our objective, aim, or plan. But what I love about this word is that it has another, wildly different meaning that also applies. As a noun, *intention* is a medical term that refers to the healing process of a wound. I love the idea of combining both definitions—to think of our "intention" as a plan of healing. To move toward unity, we must work to first understand and then heal the breach (not insist on being 100 percent right!). Rather than simply expressing our side of the problem, we have to step back and measure the distance between us—understanding not only what the problem is but what damage might need to be addressed as well.

SAYING WHAT YOU MEAN: The process of saying what you mean is about being in touch with what's worth fighting for, developing the communication skills to express those needs, and practicing those skills to accomplish our goals.

Establishing positive intent is the practice of assuming good on both sides of a conflict. For Jessica, that meant making sure she and her husband were able to understand their mutual goals—for life and for their relationship. The tug-of-war between them was based on each of them seeing their goals from their own perspective rather than from a place of mutuality. Both parties thought that their issue was *the right one and the first one* to address. She wanted him to make plans and take action, while he wanted her to stop criticizing him. As long as they considered only their individual needs, they would continue to use positional bargaining—explaining, digging in, defending their own viewpoint—and consequently, they would get nowhere. In chapter 3, we talked about universal needs, one of which is validation. We want to be respected. We want to be understood. Validation, respect, and understanding are great starting points when setting mutual goals. Trust, connection, and intimacy are the highest prize.

If both parties feel hurt and frustrated by the other, establishing positive intent is the most challenging part of step 1. Along with assuming her own concerns about her husband were valid, Jessica had allowed resentment and anger to creep into their relationship. She had fallen prey to the victim narrative, believing that her husband "just doesn't want to be married to me anymore."

After we'd met a number of times, I asked Jessica if we could play a game called "positive intent." I said, "I want you to tell me a story about the situation you are in right now where your husband has 100 percent positive intent in everything he is doing. I want you to paint him as the hero."

"Not possible," she said.

I replied, "Just try it for me. I want you to tell me the story from your husband's perspective, assuming positive intent. I'd like you to assume he loves you and wants to be married to you."

Jessica paused for a moment and fiddled with her coffee cup. "Well, assuming he loves me and wants to be married to me, I would probably say he feels really frustrated with me."

"OK, stay with me," I said, nodding along. "What else might he feel?"

"Um," she said, her voice dropping lower, "he might be wondering if I want to be married to him at this point."

As we continued with the exercise, we paused a few times to allow her to gather her composure. As we wrapped up our brainstorming on positive intent, I said, "Jessica, you just took an important step. You've allowed yourself to *assume positive intent*. If even half of what we brainstormed is true of Greg, I believe the two of you could engage with this conflict more constructively."

As Jessica discovered during our brainstorming session about Greg, to assume positive intent is to imagine the most optimistic narrative from the other person's perspective. Consider how you might use positive intent to reframe your perspective while being cut off in traffic:

Normal perspective: You stare at the other driver hoping to catch his eye in his rearview mirror. *I was here first! Follow the rules of the road, you jerk! I hate it when people drive like maniacs! Someone could get killed!*

Positive intent perspective: You smile and wave the other driver in. *I bet that guy didn't know his lane ended so fast. He's probably not from around here. Or maybe his wife is in labor. Or his kid just got hurt on the soccer field and he's rushing to the ER. I hope he gets where he needs to be quickly!*

This may feel like a ridiculous exercise, but it makes all the difference. The next time you find yourself frustrated or hurt, stop and imagine the best possible scenario for the other person's actions. It doesn't mean you are stuffing your hurt or excusing their wrongdoing; it just means you are declawing the conflict before it begins.

Here's another example: Recall the last time you were angry with your coworker for his irritated response to you in a meeting. Imagine that you didn't assume positive intent and ended up being passive-aggressive to him in an email and gossiping about it with your friends later in the day. Then imagine finding out later that he had just learned that his mom had died that morning. Wouldn't you feel like a jerk for, well, being a jerk? Even if you discover someone actually was in the wrong, treating them like there's a good reason for the misstep positions you for a miracle moment.

Most of us *think* we assume positive intent in others, but the best way to get a baseline on your ability to do so is with a real conflict. Let's try it: Think about a time in the last week when you were irritated, frustrated, or hurt by someone. What did you assume about them? (Remember: when we talk about what you *assumed*, we are not talking about objective right and wrong. You may have assumed something negative correctly—but nailing people in their shortcomings does not make for a miracle moment.)

After completing the exercise on positive intent, Jessica realized that her frustration was driven largely by beliefs that may or may not have been true. For the rest of our session, we talked about additional principles of engagement—the groundwork for making space to really understand and be understood. Here's a recap.

Seek to understand

I explained to Jessica that the next step in reconciliation is to assume things are not as clear between the two of them as she thought they were. When we seek to understand, we assume the open posture of receiving each other's point of view just as it has been experienced. One way to express this is by using the B-F-E formula: Behavior, Feelings, Effect. First you state an objective behavior (facts, not open to interpretation), then the feelings that behavior caused you, and finally the effect of that behavior on your interpretation of that conflict. And then you allow the other person to engage by staying open to their perspective.

BEHAVIOR: the actual observable facts of the incident

FEELINGS: what that experience felt like for you

EFFECT: the impact of that experience. The story you told yourself because of those feelings.

Here's an everyday example of a parent engaging in this exercise with their teenager:

When you walk away from the dinner table without saying
thanks or clearing your plate, I feel disrespected and hurt, and
it makes me question how you treat your friends and other
adults. Is that what you meant to convey?

To get at it another way, you can use the phrase coined by author
and psychologist Brené Brown: "the story I'm making up . . ."[1]
Using the same example, consider this response:

When you walk away from the dinner table without saying
thanks or clearing your plate, I feel hurt and disrespected, and
I tell myself a story that you are a surly teenager who treats
your friends and teachers with scorn, and that you are not
going to be prepared to have a fulfilling and loving life with
other people. [This phrasing is dramatic, I know, but most of
us are thinking it when it comes to teenagers!]

Expressing yourself in these ways is humbling and vulnerable. It
requires you to leave the safety of self-righteousness and anger and
enter into the wilderness of your own fragility and emotions. It requires
you to be open to more hurt, if the other party scorns you or rejects
your attempts at reconciliation. But it also creates the space needed for
a miracle. It moves you toward a loving, humble stance rather than a
judgmental or closed position. It allows for nuance and change and
forgiveness. It isn't easy—but it's worth it for the potential of a miracle
moment.

When we seek to understand, we are beginning to measure the
breach between us. Misunderstandings, miscommunications, and
intentional and unintentional hurts all create distance. If we haven't
stopped to measure the distance between us, how can we ever build a
bridge and move past the breach together? Breaches can be one way, but
most are two-way streets. (See pages 145–150 for a fuller explanation of

the types of breaches.) Seeking to understand is about acknowledging and measuring the breach between us so we can move toward wholeness and growth together.

Let's go back to Jessica. Her first homework assignment was to deal with a lower-level frustration with her husband in a different way. In this case, it was an argument they had just had about Greg not getting the kids to bed on time. Because she was leaving the familiar territory of using silence and criticism to express her unhappiness with Greg, she felt uncomfortable and vulnerable.

When Greg had agreed on a good time to talk, Jessica started the conversation with the B-F-E rhythm. She was about to learn how wide the breach between them was. Here are Jessica's words as she began to *seek to understand*: "Last night, when I asked you if the kids were in bed, you rolled your eyes and walked away from me. I felt frustrated and confused. I'm telling myself a story that I really bother you and you don't want to be around me. I'm wondering if you could help me understand where you were coming from."

And then Greg shook his head and laughed sarcastically. *(Cue foreboding music . . .)*

So what would *you* do if you were Jessica?

a. Grit your teeth and turn and leave the room, holding silence as your weapon.

b. Snap back by laughing yourself, raising your voice and saying, "You have *got* to be kidding me! Aren't you just the most high and mighty gift to God's earth!"

c. Throw something at Greg's sarcastic face.

d. Pursue the miracle.

If you answered a, b, or c (or a, b, *and* c), you get it. You get how hard it is to actually lean into conflict when these powerful defense mechanisms are at work. You've been handling conflict the same way for a long time. It was already so hard to try something new and now *this*. But here's the thing: Expressing yourself differently about your hurt is impressive, but it's not the miracle moment. Jessica's miracle moment was right then, when she wanted to shut up, give up, or blow up, but she responded *differently*.

This was Jessica's chicken-dance moment, something she learned about when we discussed self-awareness. Jessica's great challenge was to not listen to the music or engage in the dance. Greg's response made Jessica angry, so she needed to allow that emotion to roll over and through her while rehearsing positive intent.

Jessica was aware that Greg had felt hurt by her in the past, and as great as it would be to undo hundreds of frustrating interactions with one new technique, Jessica was smarter than that. She knew she couldn't make Greg respond differently, but she could change her attitude about it. She silently repeated a mantra to herself: *He's hurt and frustrated too. He's hurt and frustrated too.* By doing this, Jessica succeeded in staying in the moment. She knew that years of dysfunctional conversation wouldn't change overnight. Her only responsibility right then was to seek to understand—to be able to restate what Greg was feeling or experiencing. Greg's sarcastic laugh, although triggering, was actually telling her something: He had been experiencing her much differently than she intended.

Like Jessica, you must seek to understand the other party until they agree you actually understand them. It doesn't make them right and/or turn you into an obedient robot. But there is no solving a problem you don't actually understand, *and the problem is not usually what you are fighting about—it's something deeper*. By seeking to understand, you help the other person say what they mean before you say what you mean, and that's the beginning of a miracle moment.

WHEN TO BE QUIET, WHEN TO SPEAK UP

In most situations, there is a person who speaks up and a person who shuts up when it comes to conflict. Jessica tends to talk and Greg tends to withdraw. Jessica finds it hard to let him finish his thoughts without interrupting. Her job in the bedtime conversation was to *be quiet*. I encouraged her to count to ten slowly in her head . . . and then count to it ten more times. When Greg sarcastically laughed and shared that "nothing was wrong," I had coached Jessica to be ready with a response: "Are you sure? I want to listen and understand why you seemed upset in our last conversation." If, like Jessica, you are the one who tends to use more words, your great challenge in this step is to be quiet. Be quiet. Be quiet. Be quiet.

On the other hand, if I'd been counseling Greg right then, I would have told him that this was his opportunity to *speak up*. Perhaps you shut down during a conflict, as Greg did. If so, your role is to speak up. Your partner cannot know what's wrong if you do not use words to express yourself. You do not have to have the answers. It's enough to say how the moment made you feel.

Jessica needed to give Greg space to test her and see if she really was going to listen. Jessica counted to ten. When recounting the moment during our next session, she admitted how agonizing the silence was. "I can't believe how fast I wanted to speak up when he was quiet. I mean, waiting for him to respond was so, so hard. It makes me wonder if I've ever waited for him to respond to anything."

Jessica again asked Greg what was wrong, but he still wouldn't engage. She and I had discussed that possibility because we knew that sharing his feelings would be a big change from the way Greg usually engaged with her. I had encouraged her to try what we call "the buffet menu" approach in coaching. She could throw out several options, a menu of responses, to see if that would help Greg begin talking. She could mention behaviors she'd observed during their interaction over the kids' bedtime and present some menu options. She might say, "You were really quiet after our interaction, and I wonder if you felt frustrated? Or disrespected? Or hurt?" Remember, the point of this step is not to explain yourself, defend yourself, or correct your partner. It's merely to understand the experience from their point of view.

If Greg still didn't respond, Jessica might want to express her side of the argument. But what if Greg chose that moment to verbally retaliate? The chicken dance music would start all over again. Jessica might be tempted to be hurt, frustrated, and angry that after all of her listening and patience, he interrupted her as soon as she started sharing.

Do not fall for that temptation. Remember, this isn't about choosing sides; it's about getting on the same side. If it takes you beginning to share before they can share what's going on with them—let them have the floor. When they are finally ready to swing, let them swing. Dance with their response and let them talk. It doesn't mean you will never express your side—you are just seeking to understand first.

Own all you can (but not more than you can)

Once you've heard from the other person about their hurt, the final step in seeking to understand is to apologize fully and sincerely for anything that you can—but no more. You can own

> your compassion for the other person's hurt
> your grief for how a person experienced your words or actions
> your apology for the hurt you've caused (even if it's unintended)
> your desire to move past that hurt

Apologies happen as a one-way street. We apologize for our behavior regardless of the circumstances that got us there. In a healthy relationship, both parties will want to own all that they can—every single bit of hurt they can apologize for. True apologies are simple in structure but hard to give because they require us to own 100 percent of our behavior regardless of whether the other person owns theirs.

P. M. Forni, author of *Choosing Civility*, says that a true apology "should convey that we know exactly *what* we did that was wrong, that we understand the *effects* of our actions, and that we are not looking

SAYING "I'M SORRY" DOESN'T ALWAYS MEAN YOU'RE SORRY

There are many ways to use the word *sorry* as a way to excuse or defend yourself rather than to actually apologize. Here's a list of things that are definitely *not* apologies:

Scenario #1: The "conditional" apology

In this scenario, the person makes an apology conditional on why the other party "made" them act the way they did. This is not an apology: it's using blame to defend their position.

- I'm sorry, but . . . (followed by anything that defends the speaker's behavior or attacks the other person's behavior)
  - I'm sorry, but you were wrong.
  - I'm sorry, but you should have done what I told you the first time.
  - I'm sorry, but you were the one who was late with the report.
  - I'm sorry, but you shouldn't have talked back to me in the first place.

Scenario #2: The "something's wrong with you" apology

In this scenario, the speaker manipulates the situation to make the other party the problem. This is not an apology: It's gaslighting, a term used to describe manipulation used to make the other party doubt their reality.

- I'm sorry you feel that way.
- I'm sorry you are so sensitive.
- I'm sorry you didn't listen the first time.
- I'm sorry you heard wrong.

Scenario #3: The "you should understand me" apology

Similar to scenario #2, the person subtly makes the misbehavior the other party's fault. The underlying message is that it's their shortcoming or character flaw that led to this result.

- I'm sorry you took it that way.
- I'm sorry; that's not what I meant.
- I'm sorry you didn't understand.
- I'm sorry you think that's what I said.

But what if this is the way my spouse/child/coworker/boss "apologizes" to me?

If I may state the obvious, as human beings, we are far better at pointing out faults in other people than we are in ourselves. Jesus reminded His followers, "You will be treated as you treat others. The standard you use in judging is the standard by which you will be judged" (Matthew 7:2). He then told a story about removing the plank from your own eye before dealing with the speck in your brother's eye (7:1-5). And for many of us, seeing this kind of "Sorry, I'm not sorry" behavior in other people is easy. What's *hard* to do is actually become a person who gives sincere apologies.

So to follow Jesus' lead, before you worry too much about how other people are apologizing to you, start with your own internal audit. Most everyone I know (including myself) needs some training and encouragement to be a person who apologizes sincerely, completely, and authentically before confronting the other party's behavior. Take responsibility for any actions that are causing strife in your home and work. And after you've done that for several weeks, *then* you will be in a better position to confront other people's "Sorry, I'm not sorry" responses.

The way to do that is to circle back to the beginning of this chapter. Assume positive intent. Seek to understand. Explain how their "apology" makes you feel. And try again.

Remember: Start with yourself—your true apology can change the whole atmosphere of your home or workplace. And when it does, you'll be primed to help others change their apologies too.

for *excuses*."[2] It is easy to offer a conditional apology, which follows the format of "I'm sorry, but . . ." followed by a long and detailed defense of our actions. It is harder to give a true apology with no conditions, which follows this pattern:

I was wrong.
I'm sorry.
I would like to make it right.
I will do better next time.

In Jessica's case, the long, agonizing silence finally gave Greg the courage to speak. "Jessica, when you asked me if the kids were in bed, you treated me like you do all the time. You weren't just asking if they were in bed, you were accusing me of not doing it. You are always coming behind me, either criticizing me for the way I do things or fixing things I've already done. Last night before bedtime, you reloaded the dishwasher because you said I didn't do it right. You also asked me about the preschool bill even though I told you I pay the bills on Fridays. Then you said in front of the kids, 'We know Daddy isn't good at paying the bills'! Do you know how that made me feel? So yeah, I walked away and didn't want to talk to you because you make me feel two inches tall!"

Let's pause, shall we?

You are probably either cheering Greg on for finally standing up to Jessica (making her the villain) or you are appalled that Greg would speak to Jessica like this when she was just trying to keep the household running (making her the victim). But remember that neither Greg nor Jessica was totally wrong or right. Jessica probably felt compelled to check up on Greg for a valid reason, and now we know Greg's understandable reason for shutting down at home.

The question is: How should Jessica respond?

This is the moment that could change the trajectory of Jessica and

Greg's future marriage. This is the miracle moment. Because if Jessica would offer an unconditional apology rather than an angry retort, she would be changing a system that has stood for quite some time.

And she did it.

Jessica assumed positive intent—that Greg wanted to like her and be married to her. She sought understanding, not ammo—imagining what it would feel like to be on the other side of her criticisms, especially in the way she disparaged Greg in front of the kids. Before she felt angry; now she also felt sad and grieved that she had treated Greg this way.

"I am sorry," she told him gently. "I hurt you and disrespected you, especially when I said what I did to the kids. I will try not to do that again."

What she *could* have said is

"That's not what I meant."

"That's not what I said."

"I was just trying to help."

"You always misunderstand me."

"Maybe if you would get your act together, I wouldn't have to be like that."

Those, my friends, are not the makings of miracles. Those responses are our very human tendency to defend and guard ourselves, but defending and guarding only increase the size of the breach. Only when Jessica slowed down to seek to understand Greg's hurt could she engage with him where he was rather than where she wanted him to be.

Remember, a one-way apology does not mean that you aren't going to express your side of the argument at some point. But it does mean that your apology is not conditional on being understood or apologized to. You apologize based on the person you want to become, not the circumstances that led to your poor behavior. And Jessica didn't want to be an angry, critical wife and mother who used her kids against her husband, no matter what the circumstances.

What happened when Jessica apologized—for real—was that she wanted to listen and understand the source of Greg's discontent. Rather than defending herself or criticizing him, she steered the relationship toward mutual validation, understanding, and respect. Reconciliation wasn't easy or quick, but it was possible.

This one conversation didn't make all of Greg and Jessica's problems go away. In fact, things actually got worse before they got better (*chaos before order*). Greg and Jessica continued to hurt each other during some failed attempts at reconnecting, even when they were seeking healing. But with the safety of a mediator during counseling to keep them on track, Jessica was able to express her frustration at Greg's indecisiveness and inconsistencies in his words and actions. And Greg was able to express his feelings of inadequacy and rejection that were triggered by Jessica's criticisms.

A year after our first conversation, the difference in Jessica was palpable. She came into my office, and her spirit seemed lighter, her countenance brighter as she told me she and Greg were happier

YOUR CHALLENGE: SEEK TO UNDERSTAND

Now I want to invite you to seek to understand for the next day—or the next week—in your everyday relationships. As you begin practicing these skills, it's much easier to clear up a miscommunication with a coworker than to try mending your twenty years of passive-aggressive responses in relating with your mother-in-law. (That's pro level—achievable, but not for your first round). Remember, you are new at this!

Follow this rhythm:
  Assume positive intent
  Seek to understand
  Own all you can

than they had been in years. "Love is a battle, that's for sure," she told me. "But I want to battle it out with Greg because it's worth it."

∿∿∿

Questions to Consider

1. In what situations or relationships are you more likely to assume positive intent? When are you more likely to assume negative intent? How are those relationships different?

2. Do you tend to speak up or shut down in conflict? In what relationship could you practice doing the opposite?

3. Have you been tempted to give conditional apologies? Why are you prone to do so? Who could you practice giving a sincere and unconditional apology to in the coming week?

CHAPTER 7

SEEK THE COMMON GOOD

∧∧∧∧∧

The strongest love is the love that can demonstrate its fragility.
PAULO COELHO

THE MIRACLE MOMENT for Jessica and Greg came when she was able to break through years of dysfunctional communication and move toward rather than away from the hurt in her marriage. But better understanding alone is not enough when the breach is wide. Understanding only creates the environment where the real work of compromise and change can begin. In the months that followed that initial miracle moment, Jessica and Greg had to choose to work toward what was good for both of them by understanding their individual motivations.

Another way to move toward miracle moments is to become aware of the needs that are motivating others. In this chapter, we'll explore how to understand what another person is bringing to the table—their needs and their strengths—and how to move toward compromise through your commitment. This works in every relationship, from friendship to marriage to work—as Gary, a client of mine, discovered that he needed to use his influence to bring about positive change in his company.

Playing It Nice—and Safe

Gary stared wearily at his computer screen. It was 6 p.m. on a Thursday, and he was trying to summon up the strength to answer one of the seemingly endless emails from coworkers and donors that piled up unceasingly. It had been a hard day. He had been late to his first meeting with his nonprofit's senior leadership because his car was having trouble again. When he walked into the room, he noticed his boss's frown and raised eyebrows before he looked away and went back to his notes. The discussion was long and circular, with multiple opinions expressed but little progress toward any solutions. Meetings like that made Gary want to walk out of the building and never come back.

Of course, the meeting wasn't the real meeting—the important decisions were made afterward. That's when he found himself playing mediator between several members of the leadership team, who acted polite in their meetings and then disparaged one another behind their backs—in private, in his office. He was tired of refereeing, of being the one holding together a team that was obviously unhappy, resentful, and confused.

On the other hand, Jason, Gary's boss, liked to "stay out of it." After that morning's two-hour meeting, Jason decreed a unilateral decision via email. Then he left for an offsite meeting, leaving Gary to handle the wreckage of the team's reaction to Jason's decree. Looking at the emails from his team made Gary's heart sink. He didn't know how much longer he could keep everyone "playing nice." The way things were going, he might be the first one out the door.

Gary wasn't sure when his workplace had become so difficult and tense. When Jason had invited Gary and a small group of other enthusiastic, albeit naive friends to start building this nonprofit, it felt as if anything were possible. Teamwork, vision, and creativity were abundant. In those early days, finding enough resources was a challenge—and one that Gary particularly liked to meet. He loved getting together with people, discovering what made them tick, and then inviting them to give to the big vision of the nonprofit service agency. He was proud of the way he had cultivated great relationships with donors, which had made all the difference in the early days.

Fast-forward ten years, and Gary felt like he had nothing to show for his hard work—except a mountain of emails, a string of disappointed donors, and a fractured senior team.

What changed everything was success, or so it seemed. It didn't happen overnight, of course. There were great growth years in the middle, a period when he had loved helping the team develop more programs and reach more people. Sure, there had been some bumps along the way. Sometimes he rushed ahead without involving everyone. He usually just apologized and moved on, but deep inside he knew that he often operated independently from the team because they asked so many questions and put so many stipulations on how he worked with donors. If he was honest with himself, he had been feeling resentful about it for a while. Somehow it had seemed easier to charm everyone and do his own thing rather than risk upsetting people. But in the past few years, he felt as if nobody trusted him anymore to do what he was good at—cultivate new donors and build relationships with existing ones. Instead, he had to, as he'd been instructed, "play nice" and keep the leadership team, the board, and the donors happy while his boss guided the ship.

Gary opened yet another email. The more he thought about the day, the more depressed he felt. How in the world had his work life gotten this far off track? And would this be his fate for the rest of his career? Or would he walk away from the vision he'd been carrying for so long? The thought was so dark that it made him wince. He closed his computer screen and flipped off the light. As he trudged out to his car, he knew all of those emails—and the conflict they represented—would be waiting for him the next day right where he left off.

Gary, Jessica, and Our Basic Human Needs

In the last chapter, we saw that Jessica knew her marriage was crumbling but didn't know how to move forward. She was open about the conflict with her husband, but she had to fight to better understand Greg before she could expect him to try to understand her. Many of us can resonate with Jessica or Greg. We feel stuck in a relationship where we know there is tension but we don't know—or don't want to understand—how our actions are impacting the narratives of the people around us.

Like Jessica, Gary felt frustrated and confused—but what worked for Jessica wouldn't be enough for Gary. As a people person who prided himself on his empathy, his ability to connect, and his intuition about when he should seek understanding and forgiveness, he already listened well to the needs of others. But underneath his deferential nature was a sinister force that threatened to undermine his gifts and his career. That force was fear, which is deeply at work in people who withdraw from necessary conversations as well as people who snap or strike when conflict arises.

Fear is a chameleon, disguising itself in many forms. Fear can look like withdrawal, or it can look like anger. People who can't trust anyone may be controlled by fear, as can people who trust everyone too easily. Fear makes us overattach, underattach, and detach altogether from other people. What fear does best is keep us isolated, reinforcing whatever narrative we fear most. It generally stems from a desire to protect ourselves, often because of wounds we've suffered in the past. To move past it, we must cling to a vision for something greater and truer. But to get there, we must, as Brené Brown says, be willing to rumble.[1] And changing the way we express ourselves when things aren't right—that requires rumbling with fear.

Why Conflict Is So Scary

We have talked about how to interpret your feelings and what those feelings can teach you about your situation. But just understanding your feelings accurately isn't going to automatically make you better at conflict!

I met Gary after a board member of his organization offered to provide coaching for senior leaders. Gary was the only one who took him up on his offer. When Gary called me to set up our first session, he immediately put me at ease. He was likable and laughed easily. Gary told me about his past success and enjoyment on the job, and he didn't give me much reason for his call other than doing the board member a favor.

But knowing that the obvious problem isn't usually the actual problem, I inquired about the rest of the organizational culture—and that's when I discovered Gary's disappointment and frustration with the team and his place on it. What struck me was his ability to name *some* of his feelings while completely avoiding an obvious and important dynamic at play: Gary was scared. Despite his obvious impact and long tenure, something was keeping Gary from believing that he could influence change and confront the unhealthy behavior of his team of peers and his boss. Gary was dying a slow leadership death—forfeiting his own power and soul in order to "play nice."

At the most human level, Gary needed to rumble with that fear, and it's a fight that's not won easily. Our fears are rooted in vulnerable places, and detaching our current situation from those past places of exposure can be hard work. But because fear always makes us shrink back, it's also a thief. When we live in fear, we allow our influence, our contribution, and our legacy to be stolen from those who need it. As long as we let fear manage a relationship, a job, or our leadership, we will be less than who we were intended to be. In order for Gary to bring the fullness of his influence to bear in the organization that he built, he would need to begin to recognize his own fear signals as well as those of others. His work would be to detach his identity from his performance and defuse his fear with vision. In doing so, Gary had the opportunity not only to change the course of his leadership legacy but also to change the future of those around him.

In addition to his inability to see how fear was holding him back, Gary was not in touch with his greatest weapon: his leadership. He was a natural influencer of people. He was kind and amiable, self-deferential and empathetic. In fact, he knew so much about how tense and unhappy the team was because he knew intuitively how to create a *personal environment of safety.* When people came to talk to him, they knew he was safe. He was an active listener. He was naturally skilled at conveying positive intent, something Jessica had to work on to better connect with Greg.

But because people saw Gary as a safe sounding board, he was also the one who knew things were not well on the team. By our third phone call, Gary admitted his misery at the dilemma he found himself in. As a leader, he had a difficult choice. He could continue to be the safe place for everyone to dump their problems and concerns, or he could step up and respond to what he saw happening around him. Both options sounded miserable. He knew he couldn't stay in the role of protector much longer—that's what had him so discouraged. But he was also deeply afraid of the consequences of speaking up. And until Gary dealt with his own fear, he would stay stuck and miserable—and the organization would stay stuck and miserable as well. Eleanor Roosevelt once said, "You gain strength, courage and confidence by every experience in which you really stop to look fear in the face. . . . You must do the thing you think you cannot do."[2] Gary's fear-in-the-face moment was upon him.

In order to move forward, we settled on one "small is big" challenge for Gary: seeking the common good. Seeking the common good is about knowing how to defang fear and find mutual, agreed-upon needs that allow relationships to move forward together.

The task ahead of Gary was a tough one. Not only did he need to deal with his own deep-seated fears, but he would have to become perceptive about how other people's fears were influencing the organizational culture. If an environment does not feel safe, it won't bring out the best in either party, and true conflict resolution can't occur.

Gary needed to understand how to find mutual commitment around a greater good—something both parties wanted. That greater good would create the energy needed to address and manage fear—his own and that of others.

The Worst-Case-Scenario Game

Although fear loves to stay invisible, it's usually close to the surface of the tension and problems in relationships. It's easy to tap into how fear is in play with one simple question: What's the worst-case scenario (WCS) you can imagine here?

The WCS game allows us to bring the darkness out into the light, where we can deal with it. The WCS game allows us to imagine our most dramatic and terrible outcomes—and in doing so, expose the fear at work behind our imagination.

I've played the worst-case-scenario game with countless clients over the years. Usually we try to keep it as playful and fun as possible as a way to get past our personal defenses, which often hide away and guard those fears. And yet, it's important to create the *very worst-case* scenario, regardless of how irrational and outlandish it is. Although I've heard some very creative WCS stories, they all circle around five universal human fears, often at work behind the many ways we shrink

Facing our fears is like removing the venom from a snake. The snake might still bite, but the bite doesn't kill.

away from the truth. Once you begin to recognize these fear signals in yourself, you will also recognize them in others. Even as we mature, most of us have one particular fear that holds on and keeps us trapped. But facing our fears is like removing the venom from a snake. The snake might still bite, but the bite doesn't kill.

Five basic fears: the feararchy

Dr. Karl Albrecht, an expert in the field of practical intelligence, coined the term *feararchy* to describe the hierarchy of human fears present in each one of us.[3] Here's a quick rundown and summary of how these fears can inform the way you engage in conflict. And although I can try to make the WCS game fun, it is not actually fun to read these! They feel dramatic and dark, but if you engage with your *very worst-case scenario*, you are likely to find that these fears are operating to some degree behind your reticence to engage with conflict.

This list is also a reminder that even our "enemies" face these fears. Remember, it is not just your fears you have to deal with, but theirs as well. And these fears drive the WCS of everyone's imagination:

1. **Fear of violation:** Fear of violation is at play in relationships whenever we feel like our boundaries—physical or emotional— have been crossed.

2. **Fear of loss of control:** This is the fear of being in a circumstance in which we feel helpless or vulnerable, or in which we might lose our freedom. For some, this manifests as a fear of intimacy—feeling restricted or trapped in a commitment or relationship.

3. **Fear of rejection:** Hand in hand with loss of control, this deep fear is about the potential of becoming vulnerable and then being rejected for a part (or all) of who we are. On the flip side, we may fear causing someone pain that leads them to feel rejected or abandoned by us—and subsequently damaging our own ego and our relationship with them.

4. **Fear of failure:** Fear of failure is about failing ourselves and others in ways that trigger embarrassment, shame, disrespect, or disapproval. This is a fear that, at our core, we are unworthy of approval or love. We fear failure that would result in something we've taken on as central to our identity being rejected or destroyed, therefore obliterating our very self. Positions, titles, status, and relationships can all become central to identity, so when any of those are challenged, we react as if the challenge is about our actual identity.

5. **Fear of extinction:** This is sometimes known as a fear of death. However, most of us do not believe we will spontaneously combust and cease to exist. A fear of extinction is what's at play when we imagine something in our life that would cease to go on if the relationship in question died. It's a deep fear of losing something precious to us. This is often the ultimate worst-case scenario—*If this person I care about really knew the truth, they would leave.* It's the permanence—the finality of an ending—that triggers this fear.

So why is it helpful to know about these universal human fears? First, when your imagination takes on a WCS, you are likely to react as if your very existence is being threatened. This is why conflict is so scary. On the surface it may look as if you are just trying to negotiate a raise. But underneath, your feararchy is activated—and therefore, the stakes feel very high. Second, the people you are contending with share these fears. They may appear guarded, unfazed, or unmoved by conflict, but at their core, they carry their own fears.

Your job in conflict is to manage your fears and create an environment of safety for others to address their fears, but you cannot actually manage other people's fears for them. You cannot make other people move through their fears and deal rationally with a situation. What confrontation will do is bring fears into the open, where you can deal with them. Confrontation will also help you shape how you define—or release—your identity from the relationship in question. In facing your WCS, you are able to accurately identify places where you may have shrunk your influence or ceded your power because of fear. And once you know whether you are living in freedom or fear, you are no longer powerless against your fear triggers.

Fear triggers: silence and violence

Once Gary agreed to play the worst-case-scenario game, we were able to identify some fears driving his choices—and boy, were those fears prevalent. Gary wasn't dealing with just one universal fear at play in his work—he was dealing with several fears all at once! Because Gary so deeply identified himself with the organization he had helped start, he saw potential loss and failure as not just a loss of his work, but a loss of his very self. His fear of extinction was triggered. Because Gary's WCS involved being unjustly fired or pushed out of his job, his fear of loss of control, rejection, and failure were also triggered.

Now we weren't just talking about petty arguments and gossip in the workplace. We were talking about Gary's lack of response to such conflicts because the idea of "rocking the boat" by speaking up or taking action triggered Gary's fundamental fears.

In the book *Crucial Conversations*, fear triggers are grouped in two broad categories: silence or violence. Gary's trigger response of choice was *silence*. He used sarcasm, deflection, or withdrawal to defuse a situation and avoid dealing with the actual problem. One reason Gary ended up on the receiving end of everyone's complaining was that their trigger response was *violence*. Violence is "any verbal strategy that attempts to convince, control, or compel others to your point of view."[4] Verbal violence looks like speaking with exaggeration, labeling others as a way to control them ("Isn't that just like the admins to try to make petty things important?"), or attacking others personally to get a desired outcome. Whenever silence or violence is employed in a conversation, it derails the discussion, making it about the people and fears, not the problem and solutions. And that kind of conflict becomes destructive, as in Gary's case.

Great. Now what?

After spending some time writing out his WCS on a whiteboard, Gary took a deep breath and a long pause. He chuckled and shook his head. "Well, isn't that flattering! I'm fifty-one years old, and apparently I'm dealing with life like I'm a scared nine-year-old!"

We were finishing out our second month of coaching, and Gary was frustrated. I had just presented him with the feararchy and identified a few places where I'd observed fear holding him back. In some ways, I was triggering Gary's fears by talking about his hidden fears! To name the reason people are behaving the way they are leaves them feeling vulnerable and exposed. And true to human nature, Gary was responding as most of us do in exposure: He was experiencing shame. He was covering his embarrassment with artificial humor and a self-deprecating assessment—not of his leadership, but of his very self. Before I could coach Gary in confronting the problems on his team, I needed to employ these same tactics in my engagement with Gary.

Convey Commitment

Now that fear signals were present, it was time to *convey commitment*. Defusing fear involves solidifying an environment of safety by conveying the inherent worth of each person's presence. It's about leaders first acknowledging their commitment to the people around them to defuse any fear of rejection. Next, great leaders remind themselves and their team of the common purpose to help them recognize the value of working through the conflict. Conveying commitment to the purpose draws everyone in the conflict toward one another with shared goals, rather than away from each other in an attempt to defend their own egos. In conflict, Gary had used deflection for so long that he had begun to doubt himself. My job was to first convey commitment to him by validating his own intuition and opinions about what was happening around him. Gary needed to look past the fear and get in touch with what was worth fighting for: the common good.

I wanted Gary to find this himself, so I reminded him of the third law of miracles: *curious, not condemning*. Together, we observed his behavior as he responded to my observations about his fears: He was deflecting and avoiding the truth with humor or self-blame. As we reflected on this response, a light bulb went on for Gary: "This is exactly what I do in our leadership team meetings. Things get tense or troubled. I can feel what's happening and I want to address it, but my fear of rejection and loss kicks in and it's like I go on automatic pilot. I see my boss getting frustrated or heated up, and I throw in a funny comment or even take on some blame that's not really mine at all."

I smiled. "So, Gary, how's that working for you?"

He was kind enough to smile back. "Well, it's not working at all. The situation is better in the moment—but worse in the long run, I think." I asked him to imagine his WCS in the leadership team meetings, and not only could Gary see the feararchy at play in himself, but he also recognized that the other leaders were also responding to their fears—with silence, violence, or both.

"OK, great. So I'm fearful and it's triggering me. It's hurting my career and it's hurting the overall success of the organization. Now what?"

Gary may have felt that he'd just hit a really low point in his career, but in actuality, he had already hit bottom and was climbing back up. Although it can be depressing to realize you've wrapped up your identity in a job or a boyfriend or your child, or that you are living by fear rather than by joy and freedom, you have a choice to make. You can stay the same and expect the same results, or you can realize that you have everything you need to change both the situation and the outcome.

Gary had to wrestle with his WCS fears before he could move on. As much as Gary just wanted me to help him fix the problem on the leadership team, he had his own work to do around his purpose and his values (remember chapter 3?). He needed to identify his own fear triggers and recommit to being true to himself and what mattered for him in his whole life—not just his work. He had to seek the common good to know what was worth fighting for personally before he could help facilitate it for the entire team. After processing those fears, he had to decide if he wanted to keep living like those fears were accurate.

As long as he deeply feared the loss of his actual *self* if his WCS came true, he would be unable to change. Only when Gary recognized that he was valuable, skilled, and loved with or without his job could he actually be his best—he had to find a higher purpose than his position or paycheck. And over the next several weeks, Gary was able to recognize that staying frustrated and silent was not just hurting him, it was hurting those around him. By trying to be "nice," Gary was not holding true to his own values—his deeply held conviction to "above all, do no harm"—and he was causing further distress to both himself and his teammates, whom he deeply valued.

Over time, Gary realized that the burden of being controlled by his WCS was actually greater than the pain of his fears coming true—losing his job or being pushed out of his position. Only when he released that fear could Gary be in a position to create miracle moments. Releasing the fear meant he could bring the best of himself—his ability to create safety for others—and use it to convey commitment and seek the common good of his organization and those they served.

Once Gary was ready to seek a new way to lead, he had to practice seeking the common good by addressing fears and conveying commitment to create a safe environment for confrontation.

Conveying commitment for safety sounds like this:

- I believe in you (trust).
- I want to be on your team (vision).
- I like you (acceptance).
- I would like to know what you think (value).

Conveying commitment helps create an environment of safety. It says to people, "You are safe to bring your vulnerable fears into my presence." It allows people to freely express themselves because you are addressing the fears that keep people from being free. When your words and actions tell the people you love or lead that they are trusted, they belong, and they are valued, people feel safe to be human: needs, fears, flaws, and all.

One caveat to all of this goodness: *You cannot actually control or manage other people's fears.* You can only invite them into an environment of growth and vulnerability. But when you convey commitment to others in confrontation, you make yourself vulnerable by letting down your guard and showing your true self—leaving you at risk of being misunderstood or rejected. You are taking the position of humility. You are saying, "I am committed to you and to this" as the way you enter into conflict. You can't make the other person react in kind or immediately to your approach. But the miracle starts when you discover that this person that you thought was against you is much more human than you thought they could be.

> *You cannot actually control or manage other people's fears.* You can only invite them into an environment of growth and vulnerability.

It's important to realize that what is exposed when we create an environment of safety is already present in the relationship. It's just a matter of bringing what's already there into the light. And when what's in the darkness comes into the light, it can be addressed. Moving fear into the light defangs it and invites the other party to grow as well. The work of self-awareness and self-expression come together to make you a powerful and healthy person so you can lead the conflict to a higher vision of seeking common good.

That doesn't necessarily mean the other person will change their attitude, adjust their behavior, or even see your point of view. But in the light, you have power again. In the light, you are able to look at the situation clearly. And many times, you will discover great compassion and gentleness for the fears that you and others are experiencing. But someone must be vulnerable enough to create the environment of safety. And there is great power in that kind of love.

Once you know what circumstances trigger your fears and understand your own patterns of response to those fears, you can manage yourself in a way that creates an environment of safety for others while *not owning their fears for them.*

One of the most visceral examples of a healthy person in conflict that I've seen was in a televised interview between R & B star R. Kelly and broadcast journalist Gayle King in March 2019.[5] By that time, more than fifty women had accused Kelly of sexual assault, as exposed in the documentary *Surviving R. Kelly*. Four months after the interview, he would be indicted of multiple charges.

Throughout his conversation with King, R. Kelly became more and more heated. At one point, he even stood up and screamed into the cameras. The "violence" triggered by his fear was plainly evident. Yet King modeled what it looks like to search for fear signals and convey commitment. She used her own self-awareness, combined with her masterful skill of self-expression, to keep the interview focused despite Robert's emotional derailment.

Through it all, Gayle King maintained her calm composure and demeanor. What's more, she treated R. Kelly with respect and dignity despite the charges against him. She began the interview from a posture of positive intent and seeking to understand. She allowed him to expose his greatest fears by simply holding her own composure in check. What struck me most was King's ability to use a calm voice and open posture to convey that she was not triggered by him. She called him Robert repeatedly as she tried to keep his focus on the purpose of the interview (seeking common good). At one point she reminded him in a measured, compassionate tone, "Robert, we have to have this conversation. I don't want you just ranting at the camera."

Likewise, we convey commitment to one another by remaining present in conversations and managing our own fear triggers. We convey commitment to one another by believing in the inherent worth of every human being, despite how frustrating, confusing, or damaging their behavior may be. We convey commitment in the way we seek the common good, believing that when in conflict, both parties bring valuable, valued opinions. Both parties have needs. We might not agree with those needs or opinions, but our highest goal is seeking mutual purpose and common good together. As Andy Crouch explains, "Though it is a big phrase, 'the common good' reminds us that the right scale for human flourishing is small and specific."[6] Small and specific looks like the miracle moments of moving toward another person for the common good.

Once we've managed our own fear triggers and conveyed commitment to the common good through our words and actions, we can move toward the next stage: inviting agreement. This is the process of finding the shared "win" that both parties can agree is worth working toward. When you can move a conflict from attack mode—where people use either silence or violence as their weapon—to agreement mode, you have made a very important maneuver in negotiation.

Releasing his own fears about his future and his identity provided the clarity Gary needed to make a plan of action for the fracture he saw on the leadership team:

1. Establish boundaries with team members.
2. Confront any problems directly with his boss.

RECAP: HOW TO SEEK THE COMMON GOOD

#1: Search for Fear Signals

Before caring for the other person, you need to understand yourself. What's driving you? Return to your feeling wheel if you need help connecting your emotion to the moment. After you deal with your own worst-case scenario, you can also imagine what might be driving the other person. What do you need to do to help any necessary conversations feel safe?

#2: Convey Commitment

Speak to the universal human needs for love, acceptance, belonging, and safety. What words (that are accurate and appropriate for the situation) can you use to convey your commitment to the other person?

#3: Invite Agreement

What can you both agree is important in this conflict? What do you share in common? Moving "against you" energy to "for you" energy might mean being vulnerable and open to sharing what's important to you in order to come to mutual agreement.

Gary realized that he was making the office back talk and gossip his main concern. However, choosing to act as a go-between or diplomat on behalf of his boss wasn't helping anyone. The first step for Gary was to shut down those conversations with his coworkers before they began and face the uncomfortable feeling of being less "liked" or "needed" by the team. This started with a simple but powerful adjustment. Before someone began talking about another person on the team, Gary conveyed his commitment to his coworker and immediately confronted the behavior; "I believe in you and want to help you with this obvious frustration. Have you addressed this directly with _____?" Usually that was enough to correct the conversation, but if not, Gary then followed up with, "I think the best thing you can do is talk directly with _____ about the situation."

At first, Gary felt incredibly uncomfortable. He could tell that his refusal to engage stunned his teammates, who were used to him being the resident counselor and sounding board. But after a week of sticking to these new boundaries, Gary realized how much of his energy had been consumed by those "after-meeting meetings" that distracted him from the real problem: the disconnect between himself and his boss. And if setting boundaries with his teammates was difficult, Gary knew dealing with Jason would be even harder.

In order to handle the complexity of his conversation with his boss, Gary needed to trust his own intuition and confront his boss's patterns of decision-making by going directly to Jason. His seniority on the team and relational equity with his boss meant that he was the man for the job—but Gary also knew that taking him on would trigger his own fears of loss and rejection. Gary was terrified of being iced out or outright rejected by Jason, his good friend. It took several weeks and some important conversations with Gary's support network—his wife and several friends he had outside the organization—before he was ready to take on a real conflict with Jason. Gary knew he needed to create an environment of safety for Jason and then confront his blind spots. In the next senior team meeting,

Gary noticed Jason's fear triggers—the times where he became withdrawn or silent. Later on that day, he stopped in for a conversation.

"Is this a good time to talk?" asked Gary. When Jason looked up from a spreadsheet, Gary noticed how weary he looked. *Maybe this has been hard on him, too,* he thought. (He was assuming positive intent.) His boss gestured for him to come in.

Once Gary sat down, he said, "Earlier today I noticed that when Diane brought up the financial forecasts, you seemed to shut down. I asked you a question about our donor engagement, and your response felt dismissive. I wanted to see if there's something I said or did that made you feel disrespected or upset." (Gary was seeking to understand and owning all he could).

Gary's boss looked surprised. "No, no, I didn't feel that way at all. I just didn't want to get bogged down in that right there . . ."

Normally, Gary would have made a self-deprecating joke and a two-step out of the conflict as quickly as possible. But today was not that day. Today was the day for a miracle moment.

Gary stepped into the pause. He took a deep breath and plunged into vulnerability. "I'm here because I want you to know that I trust you. I like working with you, and I believe this organization has a great future. And I think we both want to see it succeed and grow beyond both of us. Is that what you want?" (Gary was inviting agreement.)

At this point, Gary's boss was focused and listening. "Yes, of course I want that. And I know you do too."

Gary leaned in, "OK then. I think we have some things we should discuss."

The Start of Something New

By this point, Gary had accomplished something remarkable. He had grown in self-awareness by owning and confronting his fears. He was now saying what he meant: setting healthy boundaries around his compliance in inner-office politics and gossiping, and speaking up to his boss about what needed to be addressed.

If Gary continued on this path, nothing could go back exactly to how it had been before. Let's play out some possibilities coming out of this meeting:

Scenario #1: Jason takes up Gary's invitation to a new perspective and level of vulnerability. In that case, Gary will use the steps from chapter 6 to seek understanding and own anything he can. The health of their dynamic, and inevitably the health of the overall leadership team, will improve. Most likely, Gary's boss will need help from an outside coach or mentor to grow in his own self-awareness and confront his fears. Those on the team who aren't willing to let go of silence, violence, and fear will either resign or need to be removed from their positions. Those who do engage will release the negative energy of difficult relationships and focus instead on solving problems that are holding the organization back.

Scenario #2: When Gary begins to confront Jason's withdrawal and blind spots to real issues on the team, Jason feels threatened. He uses silence or verbal violence to protect himself and defend his own territory. If Jason continues to respond out of his own fear, using withdrawal or distance to avoid or deny Gary's observations, Gary will either have to make peace with the organization as it is or explore other options. Because Gary has already faced his WCS and realized he is capable of weathering those disappointments and storms, he has taken back his power to choose to let go of something unhealthy for him, believing that if he must leave, there will still be good ahead for him.

Small is big. Gary has set into motion a new chain of events—in his understanding of himself and in his engagement with others. And nothing will be the same.

/\/\/\/\/\

Questions to Consider

1. What's your normal response to a frustrating or ongoing relational difficulty?

2. Have you ever been trapped by the fear of your own WCS coming true? What did you do to get past the fear?

3. What would inviting agreement look like for you in your home or work life?

CHAPTER 8

SEEK RESTORATION

∧∧∧∧∧

Make every effort to keep the unity of the
Spirit through the bond of peace.
EPHESIANS 4:3, NIV

I HAVE A FRIEND who was a great high school quarterback. He started every game, scored touchdowns, had fans—the whole works. He realized that football might be in his future, especially when he was selected to attend an invitation-only summer camp where college scouts began to recruit for their schools. When he got there, he was teamed up with another player from an area high school.

"This guy threw me the ball, and it was like nothing I had ever caught in my entire football career," my friend told me. "It was like a rocket. When I caught that ball, I knew in my gut that my skills would not take me to the next level." He was right: He's a pastor now, and the only footballs he's passing are to his preschool-aged son.

However, the ball he received that day was thrown by Russell Wilson, the starting quarterback for the Seattle Seahawks. Russell Wilson took it to the next level and beyond. He currently holds the record for the most wins by an NFL quarterback across seven seasons. Turns out, my friend was right. There are athletes—and then there are *athletes*.

Just as my friend realized he was a pretty average player compared to Russell Wilson, the principles in this chapter separate ordinary behavior from extraordinary living. This is where miracle moments can flourish. It's one thing to cultivate empathy and face your fears. It's another to move forward with compromise, accountability, and integrity in the way you address a conflict. But seeking restoration is about more than that. It's about the courage to truly leave the past breach behind and continue forward together in a new way. This is the pro-level step of relationships—rare, but powerful. It is the practice of connecting deeply with another person in a way that creates new patterns of communicating and relating that are better for both of you.

But before we put these skills into practice, I'd like to introduce someone who showed me what's possible in reconciliation. I first discovered Jean Paul Samputu through The Forgiveness Project,[1] an international collective seeking to highlight stories of forgiveness from around the world. Jean Paul Samputu was born in Rwanda. He was a well-known rising star in the music scene in East Africa when conflict arose between the Tutsi and the Hutu ethnic groups. As the situation became increasingly tense, his family urged him to escape. He left his village but returned as soon as the killing stopped. By then, nearly one million Rwandan Tutsis had been killed by their own countrymen, the Hutus. When Jean Paul arrived back in his village, he discovered that his mother, father, three brothers, and a sister had all been murdered—worse, his family's killer was Jean Paul's childhood best friend, Vincent, a fellow villager and a Hutu.

In his TEDx Talk, "Forgiveness: The Unpopular Weapon" Jean Paul details his loss: "I lost my mind. It destroyed my life. . . . It took me nine years [of] dealing with anger, resentment, bitterness. I couldn't sing; I couldn't show up on the stage. I couldn't honor my contracts as a musician and a singer."[2] His friends expected him to die from his own self-destruction and began to pray for him. Jean Paul struggled to reckon with the fact that Christians were part of the genocide—church leaders had led the massacre.

One day he heard an inner voice telling him that he could be healed only if he forgave the man who killed his parents. Jean Paul realized that he wanted to be able to practice what he preached—and out of obedience to God, he traveled back to his village. The entire community came out to greet him and he told them, "I didn't come to accuse. I came to forgive." Jean Paul tells the story this way: "I hadn't known Vincent was actually present until he stepped forward from the crowd and we met for the first time since the genocide. I then told him I forgave him."[3]

This began a new chapter in their relationship. In seeking to understand, Jean Paul learned that Vincent was told he must kill those closest to him—or be killed. When Vincent sought his forgiveness, Jean Paul forgave out of obedience to and his love for God, as well as his own desire to stop living in bitterness and hatred. Once they had reconciled, Jean Paul and Vincent began speaking openly about the power of repentance and forgiveness. Jean Paul regained a life of freedom, joy, and creativity. He now performs all over the world, in six different languages, singing about the power of love and forgiveness.

Nineteen years later, Jean Paul stood on the TEDx stage sharing about how forgiveness informs the way he sees the world: "In life, we must find creative and constructive ways to negotiate conflict. . . . Let history inform you, not control you."[4] When I found out about Jean Paul and asked him to come on my podcast, he showed up with his guitar and sang a song he wrote for the occasion. "Forgiveness is for you, not for the offender," he sang in his lilting voice, repeating the phrase with a simple melody. I felt my own emotion rise up as I realized the humility and power of forgiveness. That's where the miracle happens—in our ability to forgive the ones who hurt us and then accept them as they truly are. Not only does forgiveness set us free in that relationship, it enables us to be free in every future relationship.

Perhaps you think Jean Paul must be an extraordinary human being. As his influence and art attest, he most certainly is exceptional. But Jean Paul is also human, like you and me. He knows the pain of hurt, more so than most of us. But he also learned through his own self-destructive habits and subsequent surrender to God that healing and wholeness are possible, no matter the circumstances.

We each must choose what kind of people we want to become. Will we allow a past painful relationship to corrupt our future choices, or will we do the healing and growing we need to be set free? Are we willing to let difficult relationships and painful experiences shape us and teach us how to discern good from evil, right from wrong, healthy from unhealthy? Will we, like Jean Paul, "find creative and constructive ways to negotiate conflict"? His story shows that being healthy and loving in our relationships is possible, no matter how difficult they may be.

Seek Restoration

The final step in conflict negotiation is seeking restoration. In order to get here, we've rigorously examined our own emotions (*mean what you feel*). We've sought to understand the other party, owned all that we can for ourselves, and conveyed our own experience of the conflict. We've expressed our commitment to the other person, creating a safe environment for growth. We've looked for the common good—seeing relationships as *collaborative, not competitive*.

At this point, we might think we are done—but the problem is, we haven't yet resolved anything. Yes, it's a lot of steps without a lot of action yet, but every step has set us up for the final stage! So after all of this work, we must remember that we got into this conflict in the first place for a reason. Either one or both parties expressed a real need and were looking for a way to meet that need. Now we are ready to address those needs. We've sought to understand the breach between us, but now it's time to rebuild.

When trust has been breached, it doesn't come back naturally. Working toward change and rebuilding trust are not for the timid. It takes time, communication, and commitment. It takes a willingness to try and fail, and try again. But this step is the fortifying agent of your soul. It's where real change happens. Not every relationship makes it to this stage, but for those that do, it is the binding agent of humanity, bringing out the strength and resilience within. In order to get there, we must release the past, rebuild in the present, and walk out into the future.

Release the Past

I thought babysitting for the Reed family was my peak negotiating season—until I became a parent myself. Then I thought keeping preschoolers alive, dressed, and fed was my peak conflict resolution practice—until I had teenagers. My husband and I are both what you might call "intense." And as it turns out, when you combine two intense people, you get intense little humans. Watching how they navigate the world and each other—first as their mom, second as a pastor, counselor, and coach—is absolutely fascinating (and often frustrating). But let's stay on the fascinating side for our purposes.

Many evenings, I assume the head referee position at the "home plate" of most arguments: the kitchen counter. Generally, a skirmish of some kind will develop there: arguments over chores, cars, homework, or (everyone's favorite) "who said what to whom, when and how it was said, and what they meant by it." (Try to keep up; I said it was intense.)

It's amazing to watch two kids live two entirely different narratives produced *out of the same moment*. From my vantage point, I can watch the actual incident take place and then hear the passionate arguments from both sides, each 100 percent positive they have the corner on the ultimate and actual truth of the conflict. A casual comment is perceived as a harsh judgment. Silence is used as a withdrawal tactic that magnifies the other person's emotions. Hurt creates distance, distance creates distrust, and the cycle continues.

Unchecked, these skirmishes magnify insecurities and hurts. They inflict wounds, but we often don't have the skills or understanding to discern what these wounds are doing to the other person—and to us.

As the parent, I also have to rumble with my own fears when I enter into my children's conflicts. I have to deal with my own failures, my own ways that I use silence or violence to avoid vulnerability. The reality is, tough conversations don't always work. Failure is a part of the practice of miracle moments. Yet even though that's true, what's more powerful than that pain is the reality that the earlier we learn to deal with conflict in a healthy way, the more confident we'll feel about growing together with those we love into stronger lives of integrity.

This last step in conflict resolution requires maturity—the ability to rewind, reconsider, and choose a new perspective. It's the ability to honor and acknowledge the hurt of a critical word or action with the desire to move toward, rather than away from, the person who caused the pain. There's an oft-misused verse I'd like to reexamine: "Love covers over a multitude of sins" (1 Peter 4:8, NIV). I've sometimes heard this used as a reason to ignore, evade, or pretend like sins against other people never happened. The problem is, that never works. Unreconciled hurts just stay unreconciled. Over time, they create resentment, distrust, and distance. To misinterpret this verse is a grave misuse of a biblical understanding of healthy relationships. The reason I leave my vantage point at home base and enter into these kinds of moments with my kids is that I believe that talking it out, hugging it out, and taking action steps of trust are what create health and maturity. It's not perfect—but it's not passive.

Love is an active, intentional choice to move toward the common good. In another place in Scripture, we are told that "love . . . rejoices with the truth" (1 Corinthians 13:6, NIV). It is easier to move away from hurt than toward it. Love is costly. The essence of the Christian faith is found at the cross—both the literal place where Jesus offered up his life and the juxtaposition of the sacrifice and vulnerability that define real love. Love is what moves us toward one another with a desire to heal a breach. Love is what helps us persevere and seek health and wholeness for ourselves and our relationships. Love covers a multitude of sins and "keeps no record of wrongs" (1 Corinthians 13:5, NIV) within the process of restoration, not in the passivity of avoidance.

Do not forget that restoration assumes both parties are interested in growth. Don't count out your spouse, coworker, or boss until you've attempted the process—though not all people are safe and not all relationships are reconcilable. (If you keep running into trouble whenever you attempt to reconcile, be sure to read the next chapter carefully.)

> Love is an active, intentional choice to move toward the common good.

One of the greatest signs of maturity is the ability to release past narratives and say, "Now that I know your side of the story, I'm willing to let go of mine for the sake of finding common good." That doesn't mean you don't confront bad behavior or seek repentance for ways you've hurt someone. But it does turn the conversation from *what was* to *what will be*. Now you ask yourself, *How do we move forward and beyond this breach?*

When I began to write this chapter, the breach I pictured in my mind was like a road that had washed away—perhaps through erosion or a landslide. When I imagined the process of repairing that breach, I wanted to pretend that it could be completely repaired—as if it wasn't there in the first place. Pour a little gravel, spread some asphalt and—voilà!—a new road, with no sign of the previous destruction. That might work for roads, but it's a flawed metaphor for humans. As human beings, we don't "forgive and forget." We can't live "as if it never happened." Our bodies don't forget. Our minds don't forget. We don't forget harsh words that are spoken to us—sometimes even decades later. Jean Paul doesn't forget his family just because he's forgiven Vincent. He couldn't make the breach go away, but he did get to choose what to do with it.

In this final step of restoration, repairing a breach isn't about making it disappear. It's about two parties building enough bridge to get over the breach, crossing it together, and then moving forward. We can't make it go away, but we can move beyond it. We can walk new paths that allow the painful part of our story to be a spot in the distance, one we learned and grew from. Maturity is growing through and past the breach, not pretending that the rift never happened in the first place.

As we first discovered in chapter 6, seeking to understand is how we measure the breach—we understand where the hurt is coming from and what healing needs to happen in order to move forward. Often, this process will happen in stops and starts—especially when either we've struggled in the relationship for a long time or when there wasn't much relationship to start with.

I once counseled a family who was seeking to assess and rebuild after some damaging conflict between the parents created a fracture among the adult children. In one session, the father expressed frustration at needing to rehash the situation repeatedly. In a miracle moment of daring courage, his youngest daughter spoke up: "If I thought you heard me, I wouldn't keep repeating myself." For this family, it was only when everyone felt safe enough to speak up that real growth could begin.

When we desire to move beyond the breach, we must first measure it and assess the damage. A critical word thrown out in a sibling spat is a far different breach than a betrayal in a marriage. But don't be deceived—they are both breaches. There are three kinds of breaches in relationships: one-way (me to you, or you to me) and two-way breaches. Let's look at all three options and the way forward in each.

Assessing and Moving Past a Breach

One-way breach: me to you

In this type of breach, feelings have been hurt in only one direction. In a "me to you" breach, I have violated your boundaries in some way with my words or actions. I am only aware of this kind of breach because you confront me or I notice a change in your behavior.

I once had a breach with a friend because she harbored a hurt I'd unknowingly inflicted over a year before. Either she was an incredible actress or I was self-centered and obtuse (both are possible), but however we got there, she did not acknowledge the breach until long after the incident. When she finally brought up the way I had hurt her, I had whiplash from the immediate hurt I experienced, knowing she had been holding something against me for months. I was so overwhelmed with sorrow that she hadn't confronted me earlier that I almost missed the actual problem—and the chance for a miracle moment. To make the issue about the ways I felt hurt by her waiting to confront me was to choose a self-centered, self-oriented response. And believe me, that's exactly what I wanted to do—but that's not the positioning for miracles. Seeking to understand *before* sharing my own hurt created an environment for vulnerability and growth.

In the conflict negotiation lab that is my house, a recent argument between two of my kids stemmed from a harsh word spoken to one while they were driving to school. The "aggressor" did not know about the breach until a tearful argument that night after dinner. All of us have unintentionally hurt someone and then discovered our breach later. When we find ourselves in this situation, it is important to immediately circle back to "seek to understand" *without defending our behavior* so that we can understand how and when the breach occurred. The danger zone in this one-way breach is rushing ahead and trying to fix it before we assess the damage.

Pro-level reconcilers are able to

- restate the circumstances of the breach in a way that the other party agrees is accurate,
- own all they can—apologize sincerely and fully for any action that is their responsibility, and
- ask, "Have I done anything else that contributed to your being hurt by me?"

One-way breach: you to me

In this type of breach, feelings have been hurt in only one direction—you've hurt me. In this case, it's my responsibility to assess the breach. I do this by honoring my emotions (meaning what I feel) and then asking myself:

- *Is this breach about one isolated incident or a series of incidents that I have not confronted?*
- *Do my emotions align with the actual incident as opposed to "everything that's ever been wrong between us"?*
- *Is this a true violation?* For instance, I may be irritated with my husband for talking loudly on the phone while I'm writing (not that it ever happened during our "Let's all work at home together" pandemic reality). If I use his loud talking to justify an argument about how he "never respects my space," I probably have a me-centered orientation. If I want to seek the common good, I can negotiate a compromise without turning it into a breach.

One of my clients, Katie, recently wanted to address a breach with Tripp, her fiancé. She was frustrated by the time he spent on his cell phone, which made her feel like second fiddle to the news and games he was distracted with. She confronted him about this behavior during a session: "You are ignoring me because you are on your phone all the time." We then worked through the process of Behavior-Feelings-Effect as she confronted him, and that started with making sure we were dealing with as much objective reality as possible, starting with the phrase "on your phone all the time."

"Can you be more specific?" I asked her. "How often is he on the phone? Is it twenty-four hours a day?"

She paused. "OK. Um, no, I guess it's not all the time. I think I'm bothered specifically at night when we are sitting together on the couch." (The specifics will be important later—hang with this one!) Katie rephrased her B-F-E and tried again: "When we are together on the couch, and you are on your phone while I'm trying to talk to you, I interpret that to mean that you don't care about being with me. I tell myself a story that you are probably texting other girls or doing stuff you don't want me to know about, and I get paranoid."

At this point, Tripp made the mistake of being silent for approximately three seconds, just long enough for Katie to take a deep breath and spill: "I'm paranoid because you do it all the time! When I'm talking, you don't listen! I'm worried about how we are going to handle money and decisions now, and what about ten years from now? Then if we add kids to the mix, forget it! And—"

At this point, I called a time-out. Literally. I put up my hands and signaled a time-out. (This is the beauty of being a mediator; we can referee.) "OK, OK! Let's stop with this one valid point and give Tripp a chance to speak."

Because she had entered the safe space of my counseling office, Katie felt she had an outlet to address every breach, small and large, that had been occurring in their relationship since it began. And I get that! I understand how empowering it can feel when you finally stand up for yourself, especially if you've been avoiding it and growing more resentful for months or even years. But the key to rebuilding a breach is to start with one incident at a time. To put it another way, you chose to avoid confrontation until this point, so it's on you—*not the other person*—that you have reached the point of wanting to blow the whole thing up. But love is patient and kind. Katie needed to discipline herself to deal with the in-the-moment breach before piling on other grievances. Love moves toward a person and allows space for a response.

After I signaled Katie to allow some quiet for Tripp to speak, he responded with a somewhat gentle heart. "I know I do that. . . . I'm sorry."

Katie looked at him with a resigned expression. My intuition told me they had covered this ground before. The "sorry" was great—it really was. But I had a feeling there was more than just a "sorry" needed in order for both of them to feel heard and understood and then commit to a new way forward. In the case of Katie and her fiancé, what started as a one-way breach was about to reveal the need for some additional repair work.

Two-way breach: double-fault negotiations

The most common breach is a double fault. In this case, regardless of who started the confrontation, both parties feel and acknowledge a breach—hurt in both directions. Regardless of how right and justified we feel, it's a law of the universe that when we are hurt, we tend to respond in kind. That might look like silence, withdrawal, or guardedness—but even those quiet weapons are yielded in hurt and can cause damage.

When I realize that my own boundaries have been breached, it is my responsibility to decide what to do with the breach. Maturity is the ability to confront openly and lovingly, assuming positive intent from the other party until proven wrong. Before my friend finally told me I'd hurt her, I had no way to listen and understand her point of view or the story she was telling herself. If you are confronted with a one-way breach someone has with you, make sure you fully understand the nature of the breach before expressing yourself. There is no way to build a bridge if you don't know what you are dealing with.

In Katie's case, she was able to express her hurt and the story she'd been telling herself. But she discovered something else: One of the most powerful tactics when engaging in this kind of confrontation is to assume a one-way breach is actually a two-way breach.

After Katie's fiancé gave a pretty mild "sorry," I signaled to Katie to allow the silence to remain. Tripp continued, "I want to do better with the phone, but why do you always pile on? It's like I can't do anything right. And I feel like I'm being made responsible for your past hurt in relationships because there's no reason for you to think I would be texting with other girls."

OK, now the conversation was getting somewhere! Even though Katie started the confrontation, if she sought to understand, they would now get to the heart of the matter. This was never about a cell phone—it was about trust, connection, and the opportunity for a deeper understanding of the ways they inadvertently brought past baggage into the present.

When we assume there is hurt on both sides, even if we don't know what the other side is experiencing, we'll be in a position to listen openly and receive accurate information about the breach. Remember, this is pro-level negotiation. Most of us balk at this idea because we don't want to have a two-way breach when we feel justified in our hurt and are gathering our courage to actually confront and explain why *we* feel hurt. But relationships are dynamic, and for the most part, they exist as a two-way street. And if we are feeling a breach, more often than not, the other party is as well.

Perhaps you are hurt or disrespected by a coworker, and rather than confront the person directly, you gossip about the incident with another team member. What was a one-way breach becomes a two-way breach at this point because you've stolen your coworker's right to explain himself before sharing your interpretation with another colleague. Or maybe you were betrayed by your first love. That one-way breach becomes a two-way breach when out of that unhealed breach, you treat your next relationship with suspicion and guardedness. You both suffer because of the distance between you. And this is how hurt continues to fracture our lives, long after the fact. But love moves toward the breach rather than away from it. Two people can then rebuild with actions that meet the needs of both parties.

Measuring the breach, regardless of the type, begins with assessing the extent of the damage. In the case of my teenagers, the critical word from one was interpreted as a judgment on the other's intelligence, which is a high crime against humanity in my household. Regardless of what was *meant* by the critical word, what was *interpreted* was far more damaging than the words themselves. The disregard by Katie's fiancé for her desire for evening conversation was interpreted as a sign that he didn't love her, which stirred up her deepest insecurities about being betrayed and abandoned. Katie was *interpreting* his distraction as a rejection of her, no matter how much he reassured her. Before we can begin to mend a rift, we have to understand how our actions have been interpreted so we can repair the breach at the most vulnerable point.

Now (Finally!) Action

If you've been antsy—wondering "but *how*?"—this is your moment! The following bit of wisdom is often attributed to Albert Einstein: "If I had an hour to solve a problem, I'd spend fifty-five minutes thinking about the problem and five minutes thinking about solutions." The

55/5 rule applies to human relationships as well. If we don't spend the majority of our time making sure we know what the actual problem is, we are likely to solve the wrong issue. (If your roof is leaking, refinishing the warped hardwood floor is the wrong problem to address.) We do the hard work of self-awareness and self-expression in order to address the right concern. We honor our emotions and seek to understand so that we can mend the right problems. Rebuilding with action is the way we show with our lives that we are committed to our words.

The problem between Katie and Tripp wasn't the cell phone. The problem was mistrust. Merely "solving" the dispute over the cell phone would have avoided the real issue—how to establish trust in a way that helps both Katie and her fiancé rebuild from the breach and walk forward together. Rebuilding with action is about committing to solutions that both parties agree are good-faith movements toward repairing the breach. The more severe the damage, the harder it is to move beyond our hurt and to trust again. But every rebuild has to start somewhere.

When it's time for action, we want to agree to behaviors that signify our desire for a new way to relate together. It's not that the action itself is the solution, but the action is a sign and symbol of what we hope to become in the future. When we put actions behind our reconciliation, we are saying, *These are not just words to me. I am committed to a new way of continuing forward together.* In management, we would call this kind of work "SMART,"[5] an acronym used for goal-setting that originated in the early 1980s. Even though it may feel a bit contrived or awkward at first, learning how to use a flexible SMART goal orientation when rebuilding a breach in a relationship gives everyone the opportunity to know how to win together. You might not need to address every factor in every breach, but setting these kinds of goals for relationships allows both parties to signify how they are making an effort toward a new way forward. Using the SMART goal acronym, this means we will look for actions that have one or more of the following characteristics:

Specific
Measurable
Actionable
Reasonable
Time-bound[6]

Without goals, we have no way of knowing if we are moving toward our common good. For instance, if Tripp says, "You just need to start trusting me!" how will either party know that's happening? Is Tripp now allowed to just claim any question or challenge from Katie is a breach in trust? Or if Katie confronts him about his cell phone use again, does that mean she's not trusting him? Conversely, if Katie says, "You need to stop using a cell phone all the time," is he supposed to toss his cell phone out the window? Is Katie now in charge of telling her fiancé when and why he can use his phone? And if the problem is not actually the cell phone but is about trust, what happens when the next issue arises, cell phone or not?

On the one hand, Katie has good reason to want Tripp to pay more attention to her. But on the other hand, he has good reason for wanting Katie to trust him more. Without any goals, how will either person know that they are both making progress? More likely, they will grow in frustration, have the same argument over and over, and either allow distance to remain in that space in their relationship, or let it rear its head repeatedly for the duration of their life together.

Agreed-upon action is how we say, "I'm trying to change." Action is about the *small is big* miracles of doing something different. It is exceedingly frustrating to try to change a pattern with no understanding of what will be different if the pattern changes. So how do we seek the miracle instead? Repairing a breach begins when we ask specific questions to help us set up our SMART goals:

Specific and Actionable: How can each party express through actions that they desire to reconcile? I was once in a frustrating dynamic with one of my team members who was missing deadlines. As we sought to understand one another, I realized he was receiving signals from me that I didn't want to bother with any of his questions. That was causing miscommunication between us and his subsequent procrastination. We decided to create new action steps for the problem, but each of us had our own part to play:

- My team member agreed to a check-in meeting halfway through a project to seek needed clarification.
- I agreed to make sure I was attentive to his questions at that point and to get all requested materials to him on time.

Measurable: What will success look like? What happens if either party does not take their action steps? How will we confront that possibility? In the case of my team, we talked in advance about what would happen if we missed another deadline. We agreed that we also needed to create post-project feedback sessions to evaluate and continue to sharpen our process. Talking about potential problems in advance can defuse the issue. Agreeing to elevate the issue to a manager, call in a third party, or hire a marriage counselor are steps that, when agreed upon in advance, can contribute to the "we are on the same team" mentality. In the case of a power differential, it is on the person with more power (the leader or the parent) to clarify consequences if needed.

Time-bound: In what time frame should the action steps be followed? Those that are put in place "forever and ever amen" are generally doomed to fail. Often once a repair has been completed, communication improves and the specific and measurable steps are not relevant anymore. Choosing a period of time—a week, a month, three months—and then agreeing to revisit the issue can create the appropriate amount of urgency without hamstringing both parties with extensive and life-sucking "rules" around the relationship.

Reasonable: What expectations make sense for the breached party to hold regarding the action? In a house renovation, repairs happen one step at a time. Similarly, when relationships are damaged, repairs also happen one step at a time. Particularly at the beginning of reconciliation, we want to create reasonable action. In the case of Katie and the cell phone, "reasonable" was deciding no cell phones at mealtime, and Katie agreed that she would ask Tripp, "Is now a good time?" to allow him to put his phone down and give her his full attention when they were spending time together.

> Maturity is about agreeing to allow reasonable action steps to serve as a good faith expression that both parties desire to rebuild the breach.

Was Katie still irritated by the cell phone? Yes. But maturity is about agreeing to allow reasonable action steps to serve as a good faith expression that both parties desire to rebuild the breach. If Katie decided to stay ticked off about the cell phone and then decided to also be upset about her fiancé's relationship with his parents, the way he handles bills, and his lack of interest in exercise, then Katie would not be staying true to her word. When we want to move forward in new ways in a relationship, we have to celebrate *small is big* action steps for what they are, not pile on every other grievance. If Katie were to do that, then the problem would now be with her—not Tripp.

When we set out to rebuild a relationship, we want to be sure our action steps are clear and agreed upon by both parties. This may feel elementary, but it can be helpful to write them down or at least repeat them back to one another so that the commitment is in place. In the case of my team member, we held a meeting where we ended up exchanging an email with our agreed-upon "new way" forward. This is a key component of reconciliation. Without clarity, what we started in good faith might end with an even worse breach.

Many people sabotage their relationships at this point. In the moment when true rebuilding can happen, they hold on to unrealistic expectations of each other and don't allow the agreed-upon action steps to be enough. We all want to fast-forward past hurt and misunderstanding and get to our Xanadu of relationships—a utopian place where we are fully loved, fully celebrated, fully accepted, and fully validated. But that's not real life. Real life is full of starts and stops, of failures and reboots. Real life is where we learn to give and receive grace for the effort—not perfection—we each make in relationships. It's not perfect, but it is good.

We can seek forgiveness, but the reality is, there are consequences to a breach.

HOW TO SEEK RESTORATION

1. **Measure the breach:**
   Release past narratives and agree on the real problem to be addressed.

   Engage courageously—is this a one-way or two-way breach? How will you enter into a two-way conversation? Some questions you might ask:

   - *How do you interpret what needs to be fixed or addressed between us?*
   - *Is there anything I could be doing to make this better between us?*
   - *I would like _____ from you. Is there anything you want me to do to convey my trust moving forward?*

2. **Rebuild with action:**
   Commit to specific steps toward change.

   Make sure you can point to specific, measurable actions for both parties. Confirm that you both agree on the steps toward rebuilding trust.

3. **Commit to restoration:**
   Walk out of the breach with words of commitment.

   Keep a close watch on your own potential sabotaging behaviors and connect your words of intent with actions.

The deeper the damage, the more tenuous the relationship, and the more likely the breach is to become a permanent divide. Choosing to forgive and choosing to trust and rebuild are two different things. Trust and rebuilding take time and multiple steps. There are no quick renovations and there are no quick trust builders. Instead, it takes courageous, incremental work that happens one action at a time.

There are danger zones along the way. We may be caught off guard by new waves of resentment, guilt, or hurt. We may become scared, unsure, or suspicious. We may find ourselves remembering past hurts or previous relationships that make us wonder if rebuilding is even possible. All these feelings are danger zones where we may sabotage our progress. That is why we spend so much time on the work of building self-awareness so we can release, reassign, or respond to emotions appropriately as they come up.

If we find ourselves becoming trapped in one of those places, we are prone to fall into our own self-absorbed narratives, choosing the helpless/villain/victim story as a justification for continued bad behavior. We may justify passive-aggressive gossip, manipulation, critical judgments, or distance as a way to nurse our hurt rather than sticking with the hard work to forgive and move forward. This, again, is why we need to spend fifty-five minutes of the hour thinking about the problem—with sharp self-awareness of our own tendencies to fall prey to villain and victim stories.

Integrity is about making our yes be yes, which means when we say we want to rebuild the breach, we don't go back on our commitment and tear the other person down. Making our yes be yes means that we communicate the following:

I agree that this action is a commitment on your part to rebuild this breach.

Our yes means:

I will take this action to show you I'm committed to rebuilding this breach.

We take a step, make progress, and repeat. We grow in our ability to be vulnerable, to name our feelings appropriately, to move toward others in collaboration rather than competition. Yes, our feelings may lag behind. They may take a sharp left turn into insecurity or selfishness or doubt. They may turn us upside-down occasionally—but if we can hold on for our ninety-second wave, if we can listen with curiosity and not condemnation, if we can let small actions mean big changes, we will be well on our way. Learning to say what we mean—not just for our good, but for the good of those around us—is a progressive, ongoing work as we align our heart, first with our mind and then with our words. And that kind of alignment is powerful. It's the place where we honor our needs as worthy of attention. It's the place where we seek a higher good than our own self-driven motives. It's the place where we shore up and rebuild following the damaging erosion of hard and painful experiences.

Once Katie says yes to the specific action steps Tripp is taking to show that he's trustworthy and loves and respects her, the ball is now in her court. Choosing to trust him and not pile on additional accusations will be an act of will. Responding to his complaint about her lack of trust will require creative and constructive thinking. The work isn't easy but it's worth it, because when relationships survive and rebuild through a breach, they become stronger.

Rebuilding with action is about connecting our words of intent with changed behavior. It's saying, "I will do X now because I want to express Y." It's Tripp saying, "I will put my cell phone down when you ask because I want to express my love to you." It's Katie saying, "I will respect your space because I want to express my trust in you." Love isn't love in words alone; it's words with action. As the apostle John wrote, "Let us not love with words or speech but with actions and in truth" (1 John 3:18, NIV).

Steffany Gretzinger expresses the heart of this kind of restoration in her song "Tell Me the Truth": "Without the self-protection / love can mend what's broken."[7] Let this be our aspirational vision for what is possible in relationships of all kinds—with friends, family members, our marriage partner, and coworkers.

〰〰〰

Questions to Consider

1. Have you experienced a one-way breach in a relationship? How was it healed?

2. Have you ever healed a relationship by taking any of the steps outlined here? What action was needed to rebuild trust? How long did it take to restore the relationship?

3. Why is committing to restoration for the long haul in our relationships so difficult?

PART THREE

DO WHAT YOU SAY

Words give us the capacity to shape reality, but only actions create reality.

CHAPTER 9

BOUNDARIES: SHAPING YOUR YES AND NO

∿∿∿∿

Your beliefs become your thoughts. Your thoughts become your words.
Your words become your actions. Your actions become your habits.
Your habits become your values. Your values become your destiny.

MAHATMA GHANDI

IN MY ROLE AS A COACH, one of the things I love most is the opportunity to walk beside people as they begin to awaken to themselves—when they become brave enough to listen to who they really are and how they can bring their full self into the world. As one of my clients said recently, "I don't know who I'm going to discover!" I encouraged her that this isn't about discovery, it's about *rediscovery*—the process of finding again who you were always meant to be. But this process happens one step at a time, by choosing to live with purpose and healthy boundaries that allow you to say yes, to say no, and to have the strength to act with integrity in your life and relationships.

Lindsay is a great example: I had a front-row seat to observe Lindsay waking up to her full self through an online coaching circle, which was designed to help participants get in touch with their passion and gifts. Each week, the group would go through a series of self-discovery exercises and then come back to the circle to share what they'd learned. The group was packed with power—an all-female circle of educators, leaders, professionals, and experts in various fields.

One particular evening, woman after woman shared what she had discovered about what brought her joy, what filled and drained her soul, and what it might look like to step more fully into her passion. At last the only person who hadn't spoken was Lindsay. With just a few minutes left in our meeting time, I asked her what she wanted to add. Lindsay shrugged and then said with uncertainty in her voice, "I'm just not sure. I don't even know how to complete this exercise. I have no idea what I want!"

I immediately resonated with Lindsay's confusion, since I've faced it in my own life time and time again. As the current of daily routines, relationships, and responsibilities carries us faster and faster down the river of life, we may find ourselves so engrossed in the waves right in front of us that we begin to drift from the person we once thought we were becoming. It's as if we enter that current of adulthood and then ride it for months or even years without ever stepping on shore to dry off and evaluate where we are, how we've grown, and who we are becoming.

After I asked a few more questions, Lindsay told me she didn't know what she wanted or cared about, not only in her career but in any area of life. She had difficulty remembering anything she loved or felt passionate about. Again, Lindsay wasn't alone. During demanding seasons like parenting young children, or when we've tried to outpace the speed of life for years because of our own ambition, anxiety, or insecurity, our exhaustion and weariness can leave us uncertain about who we really are—or who we are meant to be.

Just before our session ended, I challenged Lindsay to pay attention that week to the very smallest things she liked and disliked. I encouraged her to be present in the small decisions—down to what she ate and what she wore.

"Lindsay, I want you to ask yourself, *Do I like this breakfast? Do I like these pants?* And if you don't like eggs, say to yourself, *I don't like eggs!* and if you don't like your pants, no matter how much you paid for them or how much you thought you would like them, tell yourself, *I don't like these pants!*" Lindsay laughed but agreed to play along.

During our call the following week, Lindsay spoke up quickly. "I want to share what I've learned this week!" she said excitedly. "I've had an awakening! My kitchen is full of owl decor. I don't know why. I've got owl towels, owl salt and pepper shakers, owls everywhere. But I looked around while making breakfast one morning and I was like, *I don't like these.*"

Lindsay became more animated. "And then"—she paused for effect—"I actually told my husband, '*I don't like owls!* I'm getting rid of these owls!' And I did it! I got rid of them! Gave 'em away!'" She laughed again. "I just can't believe it. I am a different person."

Now you might think that declaring your opinion on owl decor is not a life-shaking reality—but for Lindsay, that small moment became the catalyst to help her rediscover who she really is. Lindsay had become progressively out of touch with herself. Later, we would dive into more of why that was the case, but becoming awake to herself started with the smallest of steps. By following the *small is big* premise of change, Lindsay began, in one small way, to reactivate her awareness of her preferences and passions so she could get back in touch with her greater purpose and worth in the world. The owls of today could become the hard conversations of tomorrow as Lindsay moved toward redefining her sense of self and reestablishing her boundaries as a person (no owls allowed).

If you've been nodding along and agreeing in theory with all we've covered so far, but have been secretly wondering *how in the world* you can start to live into this new reality, this chapter is for you. Ultimately, the only thing that matters is following through on what you've learned. If you read this book on an airplane (if people still fly on airplanes after Covid-19) or over a weekend, or if you skim through it for work but miss this part—where you learn what it means to do what you say—then all of it is a wash. It's only when we do the hard work of following through on what we've said that transformation happens. Words give us the capacity to shape reality, but only actions create reality.

By declaring her opinion on owls, Lindsay was shaping her reality. But only when she actually places her owl salt and pepper shakers into a bag, puts the bag into her car, and then *actually gives the owls away* will she be living with integrity.

> Words give us the capacity to shape reality, but only actions create reality.

When we mean what we feel, say what we mean, and do what we say (whether with our kitchen decor, or the pants we never really liked, or the conversation we know we need to have with our spouse), we are discovering (or rediscovering) what makes us unique. And when we follow through, we are claiming our right to the space we take up in the world—with or without the owls or pants we once thought we liked. Healthy boundaries give us the space for miracle moments. They allow us to enter into tough conversations with self-awareness about our own limits and needs, and they give us the strength to carry through on our commitments. When our words match our actions, we become the kind of people that others can believe in, depend on, and trust.

Knowing and practicing our boundaries is about flexing a muscle that's required for a life of integrity. With healthy boundaries, we have the capacity to say yes or no and to choose a life of meaning and purpose. Without healthy boundaries (or with no boundaries at all), we will live in fear, frustration, and resentment—and we will find ourselves drifting into a life of disconnection and loneliness.

So how do boundaries relate to your ability to stand by what you've said and act on your word? Let's walk through a few questions together:

What are boundaries, and why do I need them?
How can I distinguish between what I need, what I want, and what I like?
Do I have healthy boundaries? And if I don't, how do I build them, maintain them, and honor them?

Boundaries 101

At their simplest, boundaries are what separate us from other individuals. They are the invisible barriers where I begin and you end. Boundaries can vary and change over time and with different people. John Townsend and Henry Cloud, the guys who literally wrote the book on boundaries,[1] explain that your personal boundaries are like the fence around your house that keeps bad things out and good things in. Fences also have gates—openings where people can enter and leave. To have a boundary is to build the fence that gives you freedom to live within the parameters of your personal responsibilities with joy and freedom. When our lives have fences, we have clear markers on what is OK and not OK for ourselves and those around us. Ironically, drawing those lines actually leads to more freedom, not less. Healthy boundaries enable us to explore, express ourselves, and grow. Healthy boundaries help us keep unsafe people out and let trustworthy people in. Setting and maintaining them is a critical cornerstone of our self-respect and integrity.

We are not bothered when people erect fences around their personal property, but many of us are surprised or disturbed to know that our personal self also needs boundaries to keep the bad out and the good in. But when you think about it, all of creation was made with boundaries:

- Plant and animal cells have cell walls or membranes, designed to be the first line of defense against intruders and to provide the structure needed to thrive.
- Animals have instincts and adaptations that allow them to thrive in different environments, as well as defense mechanisms that allow them to ward off danger.
- If a deer eats a branch from a tree sapling, the animal's saliva triggers the tree to produce bitter-tasting sap and "healing hormones" to speed recovery and ward off future attacks.[2]

Clearly, God has designed creatures with the boundaries they need for safety—and built in consequences for anyone who violates them! Yet when it comes to boundaries, the most unusual creature is the human being. We come into the world defenseless. We take longer than any other creature to grow into maturity. Studies are exploring the idea that the energy needed for brain development is what prolongs our childhood.[3] It stands to reason that our greatest line of defense is not our strength or physical defense mechanisms, but our intelligence. Our boundaries are real but invisible modes of protection we create using our most incredible resource—our brain.

So what does a boundary look like for us? A boundary is a clear expectation of what you will allow and not allow with others, including the right to

- choose the emotional and physical space between you and another person,
- decide how and when you will use your resources (time, money, energy),
- express your desires and opinions without being manipulated or gaslighted[4] into believing your views are not valid, and
- clearly set out your own boundaries and enact consequences when they are violated.

It's easy to skim that list and feel pretty confident that you know what your boundaries are. But they can be tricky. Consider the following scenarios:

Your adult child wants to move back home to attend graduate school. Are you obligated to say yes? If you do say yes, how should you handle things like rent, household chores, groceries, and friends?

Your husband has been spending money on his guys' night out beyond what you think you can afford. When you bring it up to him, he says you are being a tightwad and that he "earns the right to have a little fun now and then." He is the primary breadwinner in your home. What's your next move?

You've heard from coworkers that your boss is subtly criticizing the way you've been leading your direct reports, but she has not come directly to you. What do you do?

Your girlfriend has a child from her first marriage. The two of you are getting more serious, but you are bothered that she seems to be constantly caught up in the custody drama with her ex and gets defensive if you try to talk about how to balance her parenting and your relationship together. Do you say something or stay quiet?

When we put real-life scenarios in place, we find that boundaries, like relationships, are hard to maintain. Our relationships require us to make difficult decisions, and we come to scenarios like the ones above with a set of beliefs based on our own experiences as well as what we have learned or believe about love, responsibility, conflict, and compromise. As we become aware of what we value in life, those invisible boundary lines become clearer in our own minds. Often it's when our boundaries are pushed or violated that our souls sound the alarm—and we can choose to work on our self-awareness and self-expression so we can put words to our experiences. But none of it matters if we don't actually follow through on our intentions.

One of the misconceptions people have about boundaries is that they are inherently selfish or lead to loneliness or isolation. Nothing could be further from the truth. Knowing and living by your boundaries allows you to express love—not out of resentment or obligation, but out of generosity and freedom. Boundaries allow you to use your resources in a way that aligns with your purpose and values, rather than feeling that you have to live your life by other people's standards.

Boundaries make you a safe person—people around you can trust you because your words and actions line up. Boundaries are also flexible. When you know where your fences are, you can decide when you want to open the gate and let someone in. You bear others' burdens with intention, not with frustration. You are the gatekeeper of your physical and emotional space and your precious resources, and you model for those around you what it looks like to live with a healthy sense of self. That's why boundaries—and the integrity to act on them—are the ultimate form of self-respect.

Most of us struggle with our boundaries in at least some relationships. You may be a great boundary keeper at work but struggle to maintain them with your spouse. You may be great at friendship but can't seem to enforce boundaries with your adult child. Perhaps you have a loved one who struggles with addiction, depression, or other chronic crises. Every time they need something from you—time, money, or emotional support—you are convinced this is the last time you will offer it. It feels heartless and cruel to not respond to their needs, but secretly you are beginning to dread interactions with them.

You may also struggle when you need to reset your boundaries with someone. It may be because they have broken your trust and are no longer safe. Or you may discover some of your friends drifting away once you are more assertive in your relationships. Perhaps you and your spouse are approaching the empty nest and have wildly different ideas on what the next season of life will look like. How do you apply boundaries then?

Defining and enforcing boundaries doesn't have to be scary or confusing. Much like our emotions, when boundaries are healthy, they give us important signals about how to protect ourselves and love people well. Knowing and honoring your boundaries is empowering. Your ability to honor your boundaries is what makes you a safe, sound, and secure person. You trust yourself—and others trust you too.

Setting Boundaries: Needs, Wants, Likes

Boundaries can be difficult to establish when you are confused about what you are supposed to stand up for—and what you should just let go. Understanding the difference between needs, wants, and likes is an important step in that process.

Let's go back to Lindsay. The reason I assigned Lindsay the *small is big* homework on her likes and dislikes is that I wanted to help her rediscover her boundaries from the outside in. Picture boundaries as concentric circles around you:

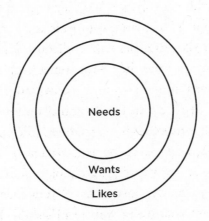

Outer circle: your likes

Your preferences are the furthest out "fence" of boundaries. Likes don't have value judgments associated with them; they are completely neutral to your belief system. You like chocolate ice cream more than vanilla. You like walking more than biking. You like mornings better than evenings. You love the Knicks, and your spouse loves the Nets. Your preferences are your opinions, and everyone is entitled to their own. A like is something you enjoy but it isn't crucial to your life.

Maybe you've known people who claim to be suffering from a boundary violation when others don't share their opinion. They are confusing likes with needs. You may like the Knicks, you may even want your family to like them, but those who don't like that team or don't even like basketball are entitled to their opinion. If you act hurt, resentful, or angry because people have different likes and opinions than yours, you might be violating *their* boundaries. Learning to be respectful and open to other people's likes and wants is a great step toward maturity.

On the other hand, you may know people who claim likes when they really mean something else. Take a classic example from a dating relationship, when the guy asks the girl, "Where do you want to go for dinner?" The girl says, "Wherever you want to go!" but in reality, she's not going to be happy unless he chooses where she secretly does want to eat. That might be a normal or funny interaction, but it certainly isn't healthy! Healthy is the ability to speak clearly about likes, wants, and needs, and to choose compromise (flexible boundaries) in the healthy give-and-take of relationships. A *healthy* response would be, "I would love to go to Restaurant X tonight, and you can pick next week!" *or* "Restaurant X is my favorite, but we can go where you want this week and we'll do Restaurant X next week."

Now give it a try! Take a moment to list five likes you've experienced this week (food, entertainment, and habit preferences are good places to start):

1. _____

2. _____

3. _____

4. _____

5. _____

Was that exercise easy or hard for you? Of those five likes, how many did you act upon this week? If this exercise was difficult for you, you will want to pay close attention to this chapter. Getting back in touch with yourself is a critical component of healthy boundaries.

If creating this list was easy for you, and especially if you find it easy to take action on what you like, good for you! A next step would be to pay attention to times when your assertiveness or confidence causes you to unintentionally prioritize your own preferences over the preferences of others who may not be as confident. (In our dating relationship analogy, you would be the one always picking the restaurant. A good challenge would be to make sure you let the other person pick the restaurant next time.)

Middle circle: your wants

The next "fence line" is the middle circle of wants. Wants are likes in action. If likes are merely preferences we can take or leave, wants are a bit stronger and connected to our belief system or values. I can like chocolate ice cream, but when I'm motivated to get off the couch and go buy it, I demonstrate that I want it. I'm willing to sacrifice time and money for it. I'm using resources to connect to that desire. Here are some things you might be willing to use resources to obtain:

- new experiences
- a sense of making a difference in the world
- meaningful connections
- opportunities for your children
- continued learning
- adventure
- status, comfort, or security
- leadership opportunities
- close relationships
- traditions

As you can imagine, when two people bring their wants into the same room, compromise is often required. I may "want" to go to the movies because I value that new experience more than staying home to watch TV. My husband may "want" to stay home because he values saving money and considers going to the movies a waste. Being able to take turns and honor each other's wants is a big part of healthy relationships.

Wants also affect our work environments. For instance, my boss may *want* more detailed information about my current project because she values detail. I may not *want* to give that information because I value efficiency and don't think her request is necessary for success. But it's right to honor her wants over my own, and because it's in my best interest to do so, I begin sending a weekly email with those details. That doesn't mean that when I'm in charge, I have to require that of my team—but it does mean that I'm going to be more valuable to my boss when I discern and honor her wants over mine.

Now let's think about your wants. What are three things you want—things you are willing to work for? (If you are confused about the difference between wants and needs, read the next section and then come back to fill in your list.)

1. _____

2. _____

3. _____

Inner circle: your needs

The most crucial and closest circle to you is made up of your needs. Needs are physical, emotional, spiritual, and relational. These are my true boundaries. As human beings, we have the agency to seek to meet our needs in healthy and constructive ways and to defend ourselves against those who would violate those boundaries.

Our physical needs are the easiest to see and understand. Our bodies tell us we need water, food, and shelter to survive, and they are hardwired to make sure we get them. If one of these needs were not met, we would use all of our resources to make sure we got it, or we would die. For instance, even the suggestion that you won't have enough water might be making you thirsty right now. (Are you thirsty yet?) We have fierce survival mechanisms within us!

Our emotional, spiritual, and relational needs might not be as obvious, but they are just as necessary for our survival. Remember our list from chapter 3?

- You are entitled to seek your purpose.
- You are entitled to respectfully share your opinion.
- You are entitled to healthy boundaries.
- You are entitled to say no to being belittled, criticized, bullied, or manipulated.
- You are entitled to become healthier, more vulnerable, more open, and more loving than you used to be.
- You are entitled to grow and change.

Think back to Maslow's hierarchy of needs. We have a need for close relationships, for belonging, for purpose. We have the need to identify our fears, our insecurities, our longings, and our dreams in relationships of love and trust. In short, our physical boundaries keep us physically safe. Our emotional, spiritual, and relational boundaries keep us emotionally, spiritually, and relationally safe.

Here's a short list of what's needed for a healthy relationship between two people:

Respectful and open communication
Commitment to resolving conflict with dialogue and compromise
Respect and openness to shared values
Honesty
Ability to seek and ask for forgiveness
Mutual support and sharing of resources (time, money, energy)
Trust—each person doing what they say they will do
Teamwork—the give-and-take of resources to support each other's lives

Our needs are make-or-break motivators in relationships. Now name two of your core needs:

1. _____

2. _____

If these exercises were difficult, remember Lindsay and the owls. Many of us are confused about the difference between likes, wants, and needs. Like Lindsay, we may act as if our needs are just likes—expendable and optional. Or we may equate our wants with our needs and therefore become overwhelmed and rigid in our approach to relationships. For instance, I may say I need the freedom to do my job in the way that works best for me. That actually isn't a need—it's not violating my safety to not have an empowering job. Freedom to work independently might be something I *want*, it might be something I'm willing to leave my job to find, but my employer hasn't committed a boundary violation against me if my job doesn't provide it.

Please don't miss this: It's 100 percent OK to have wants and to move your life toward them! It's *great* to be motivated by your wants. But navigating the middle circle of wants requires compromise and patience. When we are unsure of the difference between our wants and needs, we are more likely to be confused about where our hard lines of "no" exist—or conversely, we are more likely to be selfish or stubborn about what we think we must have or deserve.

Let's return to a work analogy to sort out the difference between wants and needs. Suppose you suspect that your boss is dishonest, and he often disparages other people. You realize that you walk on eggshells around him and feel insecure and nervous in his presence. You have a gut feeling that he's not a *relationally* safe person (for several of the reasons in our list of needs). You dread running into him at work. Although you are highly responsible, you wonder if your work is suffering because you avoid interactions where you could be helpful or speak up. In this particular situation, you may recognize that because you *want* to work in a place that encourages honesty, your workplace is requiring you to infringe on your own values. You are wrestling with your wants. It's up to you to determine if you can change your relationship with your boss and continue to do your best work.

Let's change the scenario a bit. Let's suppose you are in a meeting when your boss actually lies to a client—now you don't just have a hunch about his dishonesty, you have proof. And you don't want to cover up for his lies. At this point, your boss's actions have begun to impact your needs and you are out of your safe zone. For the sake of your integrity—a boundary you don't want to cross—you can choose to express those boundaries, knowing that your job or reputation may be at risk, or you can choose to leave your job. If you want to stay but honor your boundaries, you will need to use conflict negotiation strategies to express yourself. Boundaries in action may sound something like this:

> Thank you for including me in this project, but I am not comfortable putting my name on this document when I know the project proposal numbers do not match our actual bid. If you would like me to update the numbers, I am happy to do that and send it out.

In this troubling scenario with your boss (or in a similar situation with your spouse or best friend), you may feel a powerful mix of emotions—with fear being at the top of the list. Fear makes us shut down and stay put. It leads us to think: *Those options are impossible for me; I am trapped.* (If you listen to fear, you do have one other choice. You can choose to allow your boundaries to be violated. *But that is also a choice.*) You may want to believe that you are powerless—you are the victim. However, being the victim is a choice in most cases (other than in situations of abuse). You can choose to stay, but you must acknowledge to yourself that you are making a willful choice to be complicit in your boss's dishonesty.

Life is complicated, and these choices can feel excruciatingly hard. You may have reason to feel paralyzed—you worked hard to get where you are in the company, and you fear you'll never hold a position like this again. Perhaps you are the sole provider for your family, and you aren't financially stable enough to quit your job right now. Any of these scenarios will make knowing and holding to your boundaries feel almost impossible. But when we feel powerless, we forget that God intended for us to stick to our boundaries and defenses. And when your brain goes into powerless mode, you are forfeiting one of your greatest gifts.[5]

If you feel helpless in a situation, making one simple choice can be the *small is big* start that you need. In the scenario with your lying boss, your first step might be to ask yourself, *How would I counsel someone in this situation?* Another step might be to seek the counsel of a trusted friend outside the organization by laying out the facts as unemotionally as possible and asking what they would do in your scenario.

When I've struggled with my own understanding of wants and needs in the workplace, I've turned to wise advisers—mentors, counselors, coaches, or a spiritual director—to help me determine what that small choice might be. I once was in a particularly frustrating dynamic with a coworker. I found myself living into a victim mentality and stubbornly

WHEN TO SAY NO

- **Pay attention to what you want and need from life.** What drains you, and what fills you up? Are you a person who needs time alone to recharge? How many obligations can you hold at one time and still feel balanced? How are you taking care of your physical well-being? What relationships, hobbies, or aspirations do you want to make time for? Knowing the answers to questions like these will give you the impetus to say no.

- **Consider the cost or investment.** When an opportunity or obligation comes, ask yourself how it impacts your wants and needs. Would saying yes to this add value to what you need and want (an investment) or move you away from what you need and want (a cost)?

- **See every yes as also a no.** Use this formula: "In order to say yes to _____, I am saying no to _____." We are all finite beings with the same amount of time. When you add something to your life, you are saying no to something else. Often, we end up saying no to ourselves—we rob ourselves of sleep, exercise, alone time, or any margin to make healthy choices. You can do that—but be honest with yourself about that choice.

- **Use the holy pause for thirty days.** If you have trouble saying no to people, remove yes from your vocabulary for thirty days and replace it with "I will need to get back to you on that." Even if the Queen of Sheba asks you for tea, respond with "I will need to get back to you on that." Taking a pause allows you to formulate your no (if needed) or respond yes with enthusiasm.

believing nothing could be different. A coach counseled me to make a practice of seeking out relational small talk with my coworker several times a week as a way to break the dynamic. Those few minutes a week successfully defused my frustration so that we could have a productive and (somewhat) healthy conversation later in our relationship.

Because I've experienced it myself, when I coach or counsel others, I see the incredible power of bringing what feels dark and shadowy out into the light. Someone outside of your situation who comes alongside you can do two important things: One, they can help you uncover limiting beliefs that are keeping you stuck; and two, they can role-play with you to practice communicating boundaries and following through on them.

Understanding our likes, wants, and needs allows us to see our lives as a series of choices we can make. We are no longer bound to act and react to what feels uncontrollable, but we can step back and evaluate our needs, wants, and likes in a way that shows respect for ourselves and for those around us.

Boundary Keeping

Boundaries are of no benefit unless they are enforced. Although enforcing them takes work and intentionality at first, once you begin doing so, you won't want to go back. Finding your freedom is incredibly powerful. When you say no or do not give in to a person who violates your boundaries, it is like getting your brain back. You begin to rediscover your likes, wants, and needs in a way that brings energy and joy back into your life.

How to enforce healthy boundaries

- **Be direct.** Own all you can, but do not apologize. For instance, say an acquaintance wants to meet for coffee but you don't really have the time or the desire to pursue a friendship with her. When

DO YOU HAVE HEALTHY BOUNDARIES?

The following assessment gives you a quick check on the extent of healthy boundaries in your life:

Boundaries assessment

Answer yes or no to each statement. Don't think too long; just answer from your gut.

_____ 1. My closest relationships tend to be conflictual, drama laden, or controlling.

_____ 2. I often struggle to make decisions.

_____ 3. Sometimes I'm not sure what I really want.

_____ 4. I often feel guilty, fearful, or worried that I am letting people down.

_____ 5. Sometimes I feel like a doormat to the people in my life I'm closest to.

_____ 6. I avoid being alone.

_____ 7. I sometimes don't know how to share or be vulnerable—or with whom.

_____ 8. I am secretly resentful toward some loved ones in my life who've taken advantage of my kindness.

_____ 9. I've been accused of being passive-aggressive.

_____ 10. I find it very difficult to say no to certain people in my life.

_____ 11. I don't like to share my opinion when it differs from that of the people I respect.

_____ 12. When I do finally share my thoughts, I have a hard time knowing if I'm sharing too much.

_____ 13. Sometimes I'm tempted to get as much as I can from another person to keep them close.

_____ 14. Sometimes I'm compelled to give more than I can to another person so I don't lose them.

_____ 15. I would rather take care of others' needs than take care of myself.

Scoring this assessment:

Every one of these questions indicates a potential boundary issue. The more times you've answered yes, the more likely it is that you are having a hard time knowing and enforcing your boundaries. But even one yes is worth paying attention to. Think of the issue or relationship that comes to mind as you consider how to communicate and enforce boundaries.

you met this person for coffee before, she spent the majority of the time complaining or gossiping. You can say, "Thanks for the invite, but I won't be able to meet you for coffee. In this season, I'm prioritizing quality time with my family." *(Does it sting to imagine saying that? If so, be curious about that reaction in yourself.)*

- **Provide direction.** If a relationship needs to change, communicate the choices clearly while reassuring the person that you value them. For instance, say your adult son is living at home while unemployed. You've noticed that he spends more time on his phone than looking for jobs. A boundary might look like, "Son, I'm happy to provide you a place to live while you look for jobs. However, I will need you to move out in the next sixty days. If you would like help in your job search, please let me know." Or perhaps your spouse often yells and calls you names in the heat of arguments. A boundary might look like, "You are important to me, and I want us to be able to communicate our wants and needs. However, when you call me _____ and _____, I feel disrespected and hurt. If you do it again, I will leave the room until you can talk respectfully and calmly with me."

- **Do not use their reaction as your guide.** You are responsible to give kind, clear, compassionate communication, but their response to your boundary is not your responsibility. If you have not been good at setting boundaries in the past, some people around you are used to taking advantage of your kindness. They will likely use guilt, frustration, or shame to try to make you say yes to things. Remember that you are not responsible for their reaction.

- **Do not waffle.** When you've stated your boundaries clearly and compassionately, there is no reason to allow yourself to get wrapped up in fears or second-guessing. You do not have to compromise or change your mind. One of the fastest ways to know if people are safe is to enforce a boundary and watch their reaction. Unfortunately, we often (painfully) discover that our loved one, friend, or work associate is unwilling or unable to be a person of integrity. In that case, sticking to our boundaries may be the only way that person will grow. Many unsafe people have not had people in their lives who love them by enforcing healthy boundaries.

Especially when we are new to enforcing our boundaries, we may find ourselves swinging wildly from all yeses to all nos. If Lindsay's husband is overwhelmed by her "sudden" passionate dislike of the owls, imagine what happens when she begins to assert herself about parenting, chores, her in-laws, and what she wants from their relationship! It can be overwhelming both to us and our loved ones when we are working on asserting our new boundaries. We need to be gentle with ourselves and with those around us as we work through this process, and we need to remember that people prefer that systems stay the same—so we can expect some conflict. But with these tools, conflict doesn't have to be emotionally exhausting and painful. Instead, it can be productive and helpful (but notice I didn't say it would be easy).

As we begin to enforce our own boundaries, we may discover subtle (or not-so-subtle!) ways that we have been violating other people's boundaries. For instance, I've learned that I can often let a "crisis" in someone's life become more important to me than my everyday responsibilities to my family. I can repeatedly fail to live up to the commitments I've made as a wife and mom because of my tendency to jump in when others need me. Giving away my time to the next "crisis" demands time and energy of my husband that he didn't agree to. This is a perfect example of how well-meaning actions can lead to me violating both my own values and my husband's boundaries while he covers for my irresponsibility.

Honoring boundaries also involves learning to accept another person's no without feeling hurt or abandoned. It means learning to compromise our wants to make room for another person's opinions or preferences. These are all positive by-products of beginning to enforce your own boundaries.

As we grow in self-awareness, we become more cognizant of our likes, wants, and needs. As we become better at self-expression, we begin to find words to communicate our preferred outcomes in important relationships. But it's only when we *follow through with action* that we experience true alignment. To become a person of integrity, you must follow through on your word.

∿∿∿∿

Questions to Consider

1. In the past, how accurate have you been at distinguishing likes, wants, and needs?

2. How do you react when your boundaries are violated? Looking at your boundary assessment, are there certain relationships where you are more prone to allow your boundaries to be violated?

3. What do you need to say *yes* to more often? What *no* do you need to enforce (with yourself or others) to allow for that *yes*?

CHAPTER 10

WHEN IT DOESN'T GET BETTER

ᗩᗯᗯᗯ

Just as damaging as a madman shooting a deadly weapon is
someone who lies to a friend and then says, "I was only joking."
PROVERBS 26:18-19

YOU PICKED UP THIS BOOK FOR A REASON. You've discovered an inner desire for deeper and healthier relationships. To be honest, most of us are not motivated to change our behavior without a real reason to do so—and that reason is often pain. When something in our relationships is strained or disconnected, the pain can become the motivator to new and healthy living. But sometimes things don't get better. Perhaps you are plagued by a difficult relationship in your past or present that is impacting your ability to be vulnerable, to grow, to fight fair. What do you do when things don't get better?

Your story might sound like that of Denette, who wrote to me for advice:

> [My father] called randomly and asked to see my son with no
> notice. I said we could not meet and told him I would have

appreciated a heads-up so I could have been prepared. He got angry and told me he was busy at other times with his friends. He said he wouldn't ask to see my son again, and he meant it. His words and his tone have made me feel powerless for years. It's his way or no way. My mother has been complaining about his behavior for years; then in the same breath, she goes along with what he says. They don't realize the impact this has had on my life.

Or maybe it sounds like Lamont, who showed up in my office between church services, despondent. He dropped onto the couch, his head in his hands, and confessed his frustration and despair at his wife's drinking problem.

I thought what she needed was my support. But when it kept happening and I tried to talk about it, she twisted my words and somehow I ended up being the bad guy. I finally had to get her parents involved. She agreed to rehab, and I thought that would finally bring the change we both needed. Instead, we are back in the same patterns. I bring up something that I see in her and somehow end up apologizing for it.

Maybe your struggle sounds more like Chris, a paralegal who joined our coaching group:

I need my job. It's a terrible time to try to make a change, but the stress and pressure that my boss puts on me is overwhelming. Somehow it feels like my responsibility to fix problems that I didn't create. I have a pit in my stomach every morning on my way to the office. Every time I bring up the issue with him, he agrees with what I say but then nothing changes. I don't know what to do next.

Perhaps you long for change but find yourself following the same old scripts. If so, take heart. You are not powerless and you are not alone in the struggle. However, you may be engaged in conflict with a person who is unsafe. That word may make you think of a menacing person with a gun, but unsafe people look like ordinary human beings. They are like reverse superheroes. Superman wears a cape under his suit—but unsafe people wear armor that keeps them from engaging with vulnerability in their relationships. Unsafe people are unwilling or unable to engage with the healthy characteristics of a relationship, including honesty, empathy, and repentance.

Let's look briefly at each signpost of safety:

Honesty: Safe people are able to speak truthfully about their experiences, both negative and positive.

Empathy: Safe people are able to engage emotionally with the experiences of other people.

Repentance: Safe people are able to own their faults and mistakes, apologize to those they've wronged or with whom they've violated trust, and "turn around" (the root of the word *repent* is "to turn") with their words *and* actions, including seeking help when necessary.

Unsafe people are unwilling or unable to engage with the healthy characteristics of a relationship, including honesty, empathy, and repentance.

All safe relationships boil down to a commitment to these three factors. No one is able to do this perfectly, but relationships that are safe and healthy will value and commit to these factors with one another. Together, honesty, empathy, and repentance create integrity. When a building has integrity, it is structurally sound and therefore safe. When people have integrity, they align their emotions, words, and actions for the common good. That is what makes them safe people.

It takes strength to be in a relationship with a person who is unsafe for any reason—be it their immaturity, lack of growth, or even a season of hardship caused by a mental illness or addiction. It takes perseverance and prayer. It also takes a willingness to work on ourselves, as some of us are prone to falling into patterns of choosing to invite unsafe people into our lives. Please note: Identifying someone as "unsafe" does not mean you must immediately exit the relationship. Our relationships and lives are far more complicated than that, and the human condition is complex. All of us can become unsafe in different seasons and in different relationships.

We don't have to remove or cut out all unsafe people from our lives—but we need to engage with them intelligently. Jesus told his disciples to be "as shrewd as snakes and as innocent as doves."[1] Jesus wanted his followers to be wise to the ways of the world without becoming guarded and jaded. When we are vulnerable yet insightful about another person, we can use wisdom to discern the best way forward. One way to do this is to consider what people's words and actions reveal about them.

Yellow-Light Signals: Proceed with Caution

A yellow light is a warning signal—it's a symbol that tells us to slow down. When you encounter yellow-light indicators in a relationship, proceed with caution. You should love a person for their inherent worth as a human being, but that doesn't mean you should trust them at first sight! Rachel had just transferred to a large state university. After the first day of classes, she headed to the cafeteria. She scanned the room, recognizing no one and wondering where she could sit. When she spotted the RA from her dorm floor at a nearby table, she sighed with relief. She walked up to an empty chair, smiled, and said, "Hi, Julia. Is this seat taken?"

Julia gave her an empty stare. "Sorry. We're holding it for a friend." And with that, she looked away and toward the guy sitting on the opposite side of her. Embarrassed, Rachel not only left the table, she hurried out of the cafeteria. *So much for Julia's "welcome" speech last night*, Rachel thought.

Yellow lights should raise your awareness, signaling you to move cautiously to avoid rushing into something that could hurt you—or someone else.

We hit a yellow light when people are wearing defensive armor that keeps them from being able to express honesty, empathy, or repentance. If someone lacks one or more of these characteristics, then even your best tactics will not lead to the closeness and intimacy you may desire. Rachel had believed Julia when she told the students on her floor that they could come to her if they needed anything, but by showing zero empathy toward Rachel in the cafeteria, she signaled that she might not be a safe person after all.

That may sound like bad news, but it's not as bad as you think. It is possible to be in relationship with unsafe people—and of course, it is always possible for an unsafe person to change. The truth is, most of us will find ourselves wearing the "yellow light" armor from time to time, whether because of our bad habits, our own wounds, or our immaturity. When I snapped with Dave by the coffeepot after he suggested we take a walk in the afternoon, it was understandable that he didn't see me as a safe person in the moment. I wasn't being honest with myself, I wasn't empathetic to his point of view, and I wasn't repentant (three strikes!). But growth comes from recognizing how our defensive armor can make us unsafe. This is the first step to becoming a safe person—and a healthy person. That work is your own to do—it cannot be done for you, nor can you do it for someone else.

As long as the defensive armor is on either person, the relationship will suffer from a disconnection. Connection comes when defenses are down. You can do that by creating boundaries that invite people to take off their armor and be their real, vulnerable, flawed selves. You create that environment by being healthy and aware of your own integrity and boundaries. You know what to do when those boundaries are violated.

Jesus once approached a man who was clearly in need of His help, but He didn't heal him without first asking, "Do you want to get well?"[2] And let me tell you something—if Jesus didn't heal a man who'd been ill for nearly forty years without asking for his consent, you certainly won't be able to heal a person who doesn't want to get better. But *you* can get well!

Yellow-Light Armor

As you read about yellow-light armor, keep a few things in mind:

1. There is no one-size-fits-all scenario here. You may find yourself or others putting on this armor in a variety of situations.
2. The purpose of this evaluation is not to condemn yourself or anyone else. Instead, it will help you discover what might be behind some of the yellow-light tendencies you experience.
3. Getting in touch with your own tendencies to "armor up" will help you stop the "chicken dance" of emotional triggers so you can rewind the game tape and seek the miracle moment instead of the fight.

Where do you see yourself (and others) in the following scenarios?

The Pollyanna

When people are wearing Pollyanna armor, they are always fine. Nothing seems to be a problem and no one seems to ruffle their feathers—at first glance. I once had a friend with Pollyanna armor. At first, the relationship seemed solid—but something about our conversations was always nagging at me. Over time, I realized that regardless of how hard my friend seemed to be struggling, she never actually shared anything vulnerable. When I asked her how she was doing, she would quickly turn the conversation back to me, change the subject, or give a religious platitude like "everything happens for a reason" as a way to explain away any pain or struggle.

This friend might not seem like an unsafe person, but the problem was that she *did* struggle. She was having a hard time, but even though our friendship was clearly important to her, she couldn't—or wouldn't—deal honestly with her own issues. Because she was not safe with herself, I didn't feel safe with her. Even when I would open up or make myself vulnerable, she would not respond in kind—with me or anyone else. Over time, our relationship became more and more one-sided. I dreaded hanging out with her because I knew our conversation would be superficial and feel like a cheap shellac veneer over our friendship.

Those wearing the Pollyanna armor are asleep to their own emotions—which is a survival tactic for ways they may have experienced feelings as unsafe or unwelcome in their childhood. And emotions are like batteries in your inner flashlight. If one battery is missing, none of the other batteries work. When we aren't accessing all our emotions, we aren't able to fully express ourselves. When you have a Pollyanna person in your life, your best approach is to seek honesty and continue to invite them into more honesty through your own vulnerability. But tread lightly—because your vulnerability is not going to be returned, you may end up feeling guarded or insecure (my friends call this the "vulnerability hangover"), which can damage you.

Often those wearing this armor will remove it over time when safe people create environments where vulnerability is welcome. People in Pollyanna armor generally struggle with self-awareness and may need loving confrontation about how their lack of vulnerability impacts their connection with other people. Many times, they will need support from a counselor or coach to get in touch with their own vulnerability and emotions, and to process the hurt that had them strap on the armor in the first place.

The Politician

We all know people who default to Politician armor. Hudson, for example, is a smooth talker. His words are so persuasive that they work like junk food—they feel good in the moment but give you heartburn later. Hudson and I worked together on a project that involved lots of moving parts—and very little clarity on how decisions should be made. When we met with a larger group to discuss the project, Hudson was the master of conversation—working the room with thoughtful comments, inside jokes, and his ability to make everyone in the room feel important. We quickly hit a roadblock on how to manage an important client relationship, and Hudson naturally became the point person for smoothing over the matter. We heard nothing more about it—until three weeks later, when the client called, irate at the way her account had been handled. I went into Hudson's office.

"Man, what happened?" I said as I sat down.

He shrugged and rolled his eyes. "I handled it."

"Are you sure? Doesn't sound handled," I replied. He laughed (which did not sit well with me). As I continued to pepper him with questions, it became clear that Hudson's way of "handling" the situation was to ignore it.

The thing about people in Politician armor is that they are generally likable—*initially*. They have mastered the art of the first impression.

However, those who get close see the ugly underbelly of this particular style of armor. A person in Politician armor knows when to say the right thing and how to make people like them. But often this person has a million excuses for the reason things have not happened—and boy, are they creative in their explanations!

It's often difficult to recognize this yellow-light issue because Politicians are so persuasive. They apologize easily, they are empathetic, and they know how to make someone feel good in the moment. But Politicians also tend to manipulate others for their own gain and shirk their responsibilities. They have a hard time fully owning mistakes and acknowledging the ramifications. People wearing this armor usually get away with their charade for a long time. Only in their closest relationships—with their spouses or managers at work—are they likely to be found out. They may use bravado, exaggeration, humor, and flattery (often successfully) to divert attention away from their own shortcomings.

Being in a relationship with a person in Politician armor requires caution because of the high probability that they will not follow through and do what they say. If you work with or love such a person, you will need to maintain a patient and firm stance on boundaries. You must communicate clearly and consistently if you catch them lying or shirking their responsibility. Often a person in this armor is hiding deep insecurities about their own flaws and might ghost (read: disappear from) relationships or careers to avoid being "found out" or facing the consequences of their inaction.

The Punisher

Those wearing the Punisher armor might describe themselves as "the bull in the china shop." They are comfortable using force and steamrolling over any resistance to get their way. However, this armor can be tricky to spot because it can manifest in two ways: in abusive lashing out or in powerful stonewalling. Lashing out looks like using criticism, name-calling, or insults as a way to bully others. Stonewalling is a way to control a relationship by using silence and withdrawal to create insecurity and fear.

I once had a boss I'll call Kelly who wore Punisher armor. Whenever she observed a real or perceived slight from employees, Kelly was as likely to shout at them in front of customers as she was to storm off and ignore them for hours or even days. When I gave my two-week notice, Kelly called me at home that night to lay into me with a tirade of insults. She told me that I was not going to be successful, that I was irresponsible, and that I was making a huge mistake. Keep in mind: I was an hourly employee at a gym, and I was twenty years old. Kelly was a successful gym owner who was twice my age. Armor doesn't have an age limit.

Being in a relationship with a Punisher is possible—assuming the person shows a willingness to grow. Because Punishers tend toward rage (or silence followed by rage), their relationships are often characterized by instability and insecurity. If their armor stays in place, this yellow-light issue can quickly become a red-light problem, ending any potential for continued vulnerability or intimacy.

If you are in a relationship with a person in Punisher armor, know that their reactions to you are often rooted in a deep-seated fear of vulnerability. In order to protect themselves, they often sabotage relationships by attacking or withdrawing. Like every other yellow-light issue, you cannot take a Punisher's armor off for them. But you can set your own boundaries so you can address their behavior with compassion and consistency, maintaining a firm and calm stance on what you will (and will not) tolerate. By doing so, you remain a safe person who might just allow them to deal with their issues head-on.

The Parasite

I met a woman at a retreat once who asked if I could help her with her daughter. "I'm just so worried about her," she told me. "I raised her myself, and since she was little we've always said that we are best friends. We used to do everything together, but now she's met a guy, and I don't think he's right for her. I text her every day, and if she doesn't answer right away I get so worried. I know her better than anyone; she can be so distracted that she forgets to eat! Whenever we go somewhere, I always carry snacks in my purse so she doesn't get low blood sugar and get cranky. But ever since she met this guy—I think he's brainwashing her. I told her she needs to answer my calls because she could be dead on the street somewhere for all I know!"

I've had a hundred conversations similar to this over the years. What always strikes me—particularly when someone is wearing Parasite armor—is that I can never tell if they are talking about a child or an adult. In this case, the woman was talking about *her thirty-eight-year-old daughter.*

It can be easy to dismiss this yellow-light indicator in ourselves and in others because it's surrounded by so much care. Generally, people in Parasite armor are loving, kind, and very interested in a particular person's life. The relationship may start strong, but over time, people in Parasite armor become increasingly dependent on another person for validation and identity. Generally, this leads to distance in the relationship, as the Parasite attaches to the "host" and begins to suck the life out of them.

One of the yellow-light indicators of Parasite armor is an underlying current in the relationship that implies, "You won't be OK if I don't take care of you." The relationship is built on the assumption that one person, the host, needs the Parasite, when in reality, the Parasite is the one who needs the host.

The person hiding under this armor can never get enough from the other person. If you are the host, expect to feel smothered and as if you are never enough for the other person. You can never offer enough closeness, enough time, or enough conversation. A person in Parasite armor is very good at living in the victim narrative, and is often confused and hurt when their host of choice doesn't appreciate their concern. But the most damaging part for both people is that the host can never satisfy the Parasite's insatiable need for more, leaving the relationship lopsided and stunting the growth of both parties.

If you are relating to people in Parasite armor, watch your own propensity to take advantage of these relationships. They will always come to your rescue, which makes it easy to rely on them for all kinds of favors and requests. In addition, they will likely rely on you for direction on how to live their life—which might feel good at first but allows them to take on a victim narrative and delegate their own feelings and responsibilities to you. When Parasites define themselves around you, you are on a slippery and dangerous slope that will lead to continued dysfunction or your complete rejection of them, which only deepens their underlying wounds and insecurities.

At first glance, people in Parasite armor may seem empathetic, but they generally lack emotional awareness of how their actions impact others. More than any other type, you are likely part of the problem if you recognize people in your life with this armor. The clinical word that we'll talk about in red-light issues is *codependency*—and *co* is the part to pay attention to.

The Pharisee

A person in Pharisee armor spends an enormous amount of energy making sure they are "good." They hold themselves and everyone around them to a high standard—and they are remarkably adept at calling others out for their faults. Christians may recognize this armor on the elder son in the story of the Prodigal Son, who goes off and squanders the father's money. The elder son, on the other hand, stays home and "does the right thing" but is bitter, critical, and resentful.[3] A person in Pharisee armor hides behind their own righteousness and expects everyone to live up to their standards. Their armor tends to give them an air of superiority, and they can't help but express disappointment or even disdain for anyone who doesn't live up to their ideals.

You know you are dealing with someone in Pharisee armor if you have a nagging feeling that you can never live up to their expectations. When you hear them making polite (or blatant) judgments and criticisms about groups, organizations, political parties, and people, you will get the sense that there are only two categories in the Pharisee's mind—you are in, or you are out. Generally, people wearing Pharisee armor have difficulty apologizing, as they desperately need to maintain the internal narrative that they are good and always do the right thing.

People in this armor lack self-awareness about their own shortcomings. They live by a double standard—expecting more out of the people around them than they are able to do themselves. If they were willing to look inside themselves, they would see that they are just as much in need of compassion and grace as those they look down upon.

If you are relating to a person in Pharisee armor, you will need to watch out for any lies you begin to believe about yourself. Pharisee armor is sharp—it chips away at the self-identity of everyone else. The criticism and judgments of a Pharisee can seem so well-intentioned that you may be tempted to view yourself through their critical judgments and views.

Pharisees are great at keeping up appearances but often lack real intimacy, compassion, and connection with the people closest to them. They can be driven by a deep fear and insecurity that they won't be loved as the flawed human beings they are, so they are inherently self-centered in the way they live and relate to others. You need a strong sense of self to stand up to the judgment and black-and-white thinking that often pervade the Pharisee's world.

All these types of armor signal yellow-light issues. They are "proceed with caution" relationships. All of us, in one way or another, are prone to put this type of armor on when we feel threatened or under stress, or are unaware of our own weaknesses in the way we love and relate. But when we recognize this armor in someone else, we need to slow down and check our own boundaries.

Our default should always be to deal with people as if they are healthy and capable, while keeping an eye out for any armor that will inhibit our ability to trust them. Love and trust are two different things. We can love people for their inherent worth, but trust is earned over time. And when we see yellow-light indicators, we should slow down and test the waters before jumping in with both feet. When we are self-aware and follow the steps for deeper relationship and conversation, we are inviting people to take off their armor and grow in connection and vulnerability. It's an invitation—not a mandate.

When we see yellow lights, we can create the invitation and the environment of safety—while also being aware that a person might not be able or willing to reciprocate. We can love them, but we might not trust them on a deeper level of connection. We can love them, but when the yellow light slows us down, we might take caution when trusting them as a business partner, best friend, or life partner. Yellow lights can become either red lights or green lights. But you won't know what that yellow light is telling you about others without slowing down—both to ensure they earn your trust and to see how they respond to your boundaries.

But what about mental illness?

Having an understanding of and compassion for another person's inability to be in a healthy relationship is difficult. Some of us struggle with family members, spouses, and children who have long-term and chronic issues with anxiety, depression, or substance use disorder that make the idea of a healthy relationship seem impossible. But even then, we are invited to a life of flourishing and health. Understanding our own boundaries will help us become a safe and welcoming place even for those who are weak, unsure, or unwell.

Without a doubt, living with, working with, or loving a person with mental illness requires an enormous amount of compassion, strength, and self-care. There is not enough room here to sufficiently address this complicated issue, but I want to offer a way forward if this is your situation. I would break up these challenging relationships into two categories:

1. People who are struggling but want to be different
2. People who are struggling but want to stay the same or don't feel they need to change

In the broadest sense, people with psychological disorders are considered either egodystonic or egosyntonic. Those who are egodystonic recognize that their thoughts, behavior, and struggles are getting in the way of the people they want to be. They see their distress, symptoms, or struggles as a problem. They acknowledge their struggles but see them as outside themselves and capable of being addressed. Those in the second category (egosyntonic) struggle with behaviors and patterns over time but see them as part of who they are rather than separate and distinct.

Here's a rough example. Let's say you have an obsession with cats. You are so obsessed with cats that you prioritize your cat over your job and friendships. Eventually, you lose your job and important relationships. As you snatch up cat toys and trinkets, you ruin your finances, and you sometimes even forget to take care of your own hygiene and health. A person in category one (egodystonic) will recognize that their cat obsession is actually creating problems for them. They are in distress about their situation but don't know how to get out of it. In category two (egosyntonic), the person may be concerned about their lack of employment, ruined relationships, or financial difficulties, but they don't connect their cat obsession and subsequent choices as the very source of all their other problems! They are *not* in distress about their cat obsession. They might be bewildered when anyone suggests it might be the source of their troubles.

Both people have a problem, but only one knows that their obsession is the source of their problem.

So how does this relate to your loved one, coworker, or spouse? There is a big and important difference between people who know they have an issue and want to get help with it and those who aren't aware of it or aren't willing to admit they have a problem. Whether it's depression, anxiety, addiction, or another life-altering pattern, recognizing that some people want to get help and some aren't even aware they need help is a good first step.

As with yellow-light issues, our approach to and handling of these situations is globally the same: Create environments of safety with firm and loving boundaries. However, if your spouse, child, or parent struggles with a mental illness, you should be open to the possibility that your loved one may have a difficult if not impossible time recognizing how their behavior is harmful or unhealthy. If this is your situation, look for support. Our culture's awareness and acknowledgment of the need for mental health treatment—both for the afflicted and their loved ones—has increased exponentially.

If you love someone who is unwilling or unable to hold a job, maintain healthy relationships, or take care of their own physical or emotional health, you will need support to remain healthy. This help may come through therapy, a support group (online or in person), other healthy friendships, and a stronger commitment to your own physical and mental health. You have a difficult path to walk. But you do not have to walk it alone.

Research shows that caring for someone who is depressed increases your likelihood of negative thinking and even depression.[4] It doesn't mean that you should stop caring for, loving, or supporting the person who is struggling. But you should see this as a yellow light for your own soul.

What if I'm in a relationship with someone who is unhealthy and doesn't want to get better?

There is a high probability that at some point, you will come into contact with someone with a pervasive egosyntonic way of living that makes them hard to relate to in a healthy way. After all, the prevalence of personality disorders, which is just one type of mental illness and includes obsessive-compulsive personality disorder, narcissistic personality disorder, and borderline personality disorder, has been estimated at almost 10 percent in the United States.[5] It's important to recognize that you can love a person who is struggling with a personality disorder, provided you maintain healthy boundaries. However, it's possible that "loving with healthy boundaries" may look like a separated or distant relationship for the sake of your own health.

Although our boundaries aren't meant to be rigid and unyielding when others struggle, they are a way to maintain safety and love in our relationships. They enable us to avoid the villain/victim narrative and our tendency to try to rescue and fix other people. Healthy boundaries and sacrificial love represent the ethic of Jesus Christ, who was willing to invite—not force—people into life with Him. Yet He also went to the cross in the ultimate expression of sacrificial love. It is possible to be healthy, loving, and kind even with the people in your life who don't want to change and don't want to get better. Will it be challenging, painful, and difficult to watch them struggle? Absolutely. For the sake of your own health (and theirs), will you need to create and maintain healthy boundaries? Most certainly.

So whether your loved one is unhealthy and wants to change, or unhealthy and doesn't, knowing *who you are and what you are worth* is a beginning. However, even then, you may struggle to love difficult people, and in some scenarios, you need to take additional steps to protect yourself. These are the red-light issues.

Red-Light Issues

A red-light issue is a pattern of behavior in another person that creates an unhealthy dynamic for both of you. In her book *Out of the Fog: Moving from Confusion to Clarity after Narcissistic Abuse*, author Dana Morningstar writes about the "fog" that envelops people in unhealthy relationships and makes it difficult for them to separate or leave.[6] In other words, how you relate to the other person is not driven by your own sense of agency or love, it's motivated by fear, obligation, or guilt. Often, red-light issues occur when someone uses control or manipulation to create fear, shame, or guilt, making it difficult for others to form their own opinion, stand up for themselves, or act in any way other than what the red-light person wants.

Such behavior traits do exist in people with personality disorders, but not exclusively. Anyone (including you and me!) can behave in a toxic way, and all behavior exists on a spectrum. Morningstar explains when behaviors become red-light issues: "It's not necessarily the traits themselves that are the problem, it's the degree, frequency, and a person's unwillingness to change these traits that is the problem."[7]

Often the only way to distinguish yellow-light issues from red-light issues is by adopting healthy, empowering stances for ourselves—both in the way we treat others and in how we tolerate being treated. When we do, we may discover that some of the key people around us are unwilling or unable to meet us on healthy ground. They may not respond well to our boundaries.

What's funny about our boundaries is that when we are in unhealthy relationships, we desperately want approval and validation *from those same unsafe people* for our healthy choices. But people who have benefited from our inability to stand up for ourselves will not be happy when we begin setting limits. They will be frustrated, hurt, and confused by those boundaries, particularly if they are close family members or friends. If we've been living by their expectations, they may find it disconcerting when we change the rules.

Yet striving for a healthy, loving relationship is good for both parties, even if it doesn't feel good right away. As you begin practicing *meaning what you feel* and *saying what you mean*, look out for these red-light issues:

Narcissistic tendencies

People with these tendencies view themselves as "larger than life"—and they live as if their lives are truly more important than anyone else's. They have an excessive need for admiration and approval, a sense of self-importance to the detriment of others, a lack of empathy, and an intolerance to those who question or confront their views or behaviors.

To get a sense of the narcissist mindset, hang out with some three-year-olds. They think the world revolves around them. They hold unreasonable expectations of other people, and they lack empathy. This is a normal stage of development. The problem comes when those three-year-olds grow up to amass power, wealth, and resources without ever maturing emotionally.

Narcissists often have one standard for themselves and a different one for everyone around them. They don't play by their own rules because rules don't apply to them. Whether they are simply self-centered, have narcissistic tendencies, or have a full-blown personality disorder, they want all the power. Such relationships aren't healthy because they are one-sided. Only one person's views, preferences, and opinions are allowed; other people are ridiculed, bullied, or belittled into believing their own needs and opinions are not valid.

When we picture an abusive relationship, we often picture a battered woman or a defenseless child. But abuse can occur within friendships, work relationships, or extended families. I've seen these red-light tendencies in men, women, community leaders, church leaders, and parents. For example, I've helped several clients heal from abusive female friendships. Relationships become abusive when people use their power to control the other people, whether physically, emotionally, or mentally.

Gaslighting

The term *gaslighting* has come into common usage recently and is an umbrella word for a form of emotional abuse that causes recipients to begin questioning their own sense of what is healthy and normal. Gaslighting is about minimizing or editing other people's experience, telling them what they think or feel. A somewhat innocuous version of this can happen between children and their parents:

Child: "I'm scared of that dog."
Father: "No, you aren't."

Once again, the above interaction may be harmless (although as a parent I don't recommend it!), but when that dad also treats grown-ups that way, it's a red light. In grown-up gaslighting, a person systematically brings into question the thoughts or emotions of other people, causing them to doubt their ability to interpret reality. A gaslighter will use lying, denial, criticism, and "spin" to somehow project all the problems in a relationship back onto the other party.

One of the signals that you've been in or were raised in an environment of narcissism or gaslighting can be in what you've defended, explained away, or minimized in your life. If you have experienced habitual manipulation, covering up, and shame, your first reaction to reading about these tactics may be to distance yourself from the possibility that they could be true for you! Just remember where we started this chapter: The foundations of healthy relationships are based in honesty, empathy, and repentance.

All of us have been—or are in—relationships that lack one or more of these qualities. The problem is not being in the relationships—it's what we expect from them. People who systemically and consistently lack these values over time are incapable of meeting your emotional needs in the way you were designed to be loved. And so if your closest relationships (marriage, work, family) involve unsafe people, I want you to know that there is more for you than this.

You are entitled to mutually beneficial relationships. You are allowed to stand up for what's healthy and normal. You can draw boundaries, and if they are repeatedly violated, you can remove yourself from the situation or relationship. Love is not abusive. Love is not found in one-way relationships where you give and don't receive. You do not have to leave a red-light relationship—but in order to grow, you will need boundaries and a new definition of healthy. It's possible that when you change, the other party will no longer want to be with you. But that isn't about you. It's about them. All of us are allowed to choose health, safety, love, and respectful relationships, regardless of what we were taught growing up, what relationships we've been in, or what we've endured in the past.

One of the most challenging parts of difficult relationships is knowing how to grow through them without taking all the blame or fault upon ourselves. Rather than asking, "Why did this relationship fail?" ask, "How can I grow?" One way to do that is by looking inside ourselves to understand why we may be attracted to people who manipulate our good intentions. This red-light issue is known as codependency.

Codependency

Codependency is the red-light version of Parasite armor. A codependent relationship is one in which a person validates their own worth through the way they care for someone else, generally someone who requires help because they can't manage on their own or manipulates the other for their support. A person who experiences codependency wraps the feelings and life of their partner into their own feelings and validation. Again, a parental analogy might help here. When a baby is in utero, the mother and child are separate, but still one. The child cannot exist without the mother. Although the child is a separate being with their own systems of life, they are also "codependent" on the mother for their existence. Outside of the womb, codependency is an unhealthy attachment that leads someone to feel as if they would cease to exist if they weren't caring for the other person.

A codependent is attracted to a partner who either manipulates or controls them to carry the partner's load in life—to the detriment of both parties. People with these tendencies often find themselves attracted to "rescue" cases. They may align themselves to people they view as projects that need fixing or controlling. Because codependent people find identity in their ability to help, protect, support, or nurture another person, they struggle to engage in two-way relationships that require mutual vulnerability and responsibility. They may place a high value on loyalty and commitment, even when that loyalty keeps them in an unhealthy or abusive relationship, or they may have an over-developed religiosity that leads them to believe that they must "love at all costs." The ironic thing about this kind of love is that it's actually harmful to both parties. The person who doesn't carry their own load isn't required to grow and live in healthy, mutually sacrificing love. And the codependent person is so distracted by caring for their partner's needs that they are able to avoid their own fears of abandonment, rejection, or inadequacy.

It is sometimes good to *expend* ourselves for the sake of others. But in codependency, we *expire* ourselves for the sake of others. A codependent person will use all of their energy to keep their part-ner in a position where they need them or assume they need them. This can look like controlling behavior, needy clinging, or a helpless/victim attitude toward life that compels us to want to take charge and make decisions for the other person. However, meeting their demands only exacerbates the problem. As the cycle continues, a person suffering from codependency will continue to define themselves by their relationship rather than their own sense of what they are worth and what they need.

Taking Off Your Armor

Nobody likes the idea that they may struggle with one of these yellow-light or red-light issues. But as with all growth, the first step is awareness. Each of us may display shades of these dysfunctional patterns at times, but real growth comes when we acknowledge and address them.

Some of us have worn our armor for so long that we have forgotten that we are separate from those behaviors. But we can change, and unhealthy ways of relating don't need to control us. Rediscovering that truth and developing healthy boundaries is the only way to wholeness. Only with healthy boundaries can we love well and with maturity and then receive that kind of love in return.

The first step to getting healthy is recognizing that you don't have to live in a haze of confusion and uncertainty or continue to expose yourself to abusive, manipulative, controlling, or dependent relationships as the basis of your identity.

By seeking to ensure our words and actions are aligned, we can create peace within ourselves and in our relationships.

∿∿∿∿

Questions to Consider

1. Do you agree that the qualities of a safe person are honesty, empathy, and repentance? Would you add any qualities to this list? If so, what are they?

2. What yellow-light armor are you prone to put on? In what situations are you most tempted to "armor up"?

3. Do you have any relationships with egosyntonic red-light issues (someone has a problem but doesn't want to change)? Have you been tempted to try to make the other person change? What are you learning about healthy conflict resolution that might adjust your behavior moving forward?

CHAPTER 11

FAILING FORWARD

∧∧∧∧∧

You may encounter many defeats, but you must not be defeated. In
fact, it may be necessary to encounter the defeats, so you can know
who you are, what you can rise from, how you can still come out of it.

MAYA ANGELOU

ONE OF THE FEW TV SHOWS my family watch together is *Top Chef*, a reality show that combines all of our favorite things: food, competition, and people who are passionate about and talented at their craft. We love watching skilled, creative chefs come together and submit themselves to the evaluation and critique of an expert panel of judges, who are simultaneously clubby and fun and terrifying and cold. Not long ago we watched the annual "Restaurant Wars" episode in which two teams of chefs create and execute their own restaurant concept. They develop the branding, physical space, menu, and food and then open their restaurant—all within forty-eight hours. If these chefs were in charge of the universe, they would probably solve world hunger and climate change within a week.

On each of the teams, one chef volunteers to be "executive chef" while the others take the role of dining room manager, host, or line cook. Generally, one chef is incredibly stressed in the kitchen and another is incredibly stressed in the dining room. Both display amazing feats of strength and perseverance as they set places and create plates meant to showcase their talents for hundreds of diners as well as the aforementioned friendly/terrifying judges panel.

And, of course, there are winners and losers. In this episode, one team created a Haitian restaurant; the other, a restaurant featuring Southern comfort food. Even I, an amateur cook, could see that operations at the first restaurant ran much more smoothly than at the second. So I wasn't shocked when the first restaurant was declared the victor, but I was surprised at something that happened when the losing team stepped up for judgment.

This was the moment—part of every *Top Chef* episode—when the losing chefs defend their decisions and explain where things went wrong. Generally, this is the moment when chefs reveal the worst of our humanity in the form of villain/victim narratives. ("He was the one who sent out my plate!" "She was the one who didn't train the waitstaff properly.") But this time, when executive chef Kevin Gillespie was questioned about his part in the failure of the team's restaurant concept, he said, "I take full responsibility for everything that went wrong." In a moment when Gillespie could have shifted blame or even shaped the narrative about *why* things went wrong, he took responsibility and bore the weight of the failure. When passion, teamwork, and perseverance didn't lead to the results he wanted, Gillespie accepted the outcome without shifting blame.

That's integrity.

Gillespie is an award-winning chef with several restaurants. No doubt he wished he could have taken all that experience and expertise to create the winning restaurant in this episode. Likewise, it would be great if we could perfectly apply the concepts from this book and get the desired results 100 percent of the time. Unfortunately, people—including us—aren't like math problems. In the economy of the human spirit, 2 + 2 does not always equal 4. What worked yesterday might not work today. You can do everything right and still suffer from relational failure and frustration. More likely, though, you'll have to reckon with your own limitations, which will take you in one of two directions: You can either fail and stuff the pain, or you can fail forward and grow.

My first big leadership role was as a fitness director at a YMCA. It was a huge job. I was twenty-two years old, managing more than thirty part-time and two full-time employees. I had a budget, a department, and a voice, but I had absolutely no idea what I was doing. Looking back at that season, I now know that my emotions, thoughts, and actions were so misaligned that I used blunt-force willpower and energy to try to succeed. And in many ways, I did—I managed to create change and accomplish some good things on paper. But looking back at that season of leadership, I know that I actually failed pretty miserably!

In particular, I had a contentious relationship with my full-time assistant director, a woman twenty years my senior who had faithfully served in that department for most of her career. She was deliberate and patient; I was decisive and not patient. She took change at a slower pace; I liked change at the speed of an F5 tornado. We could have been a great team, but my lack of self-awareness (mean what you feel) and self-expression (say what you mean) led to a failure of integrity. Our shared office became a passive-aggressive battleground of miscommunication and frustration. What could have been a miracle moment—and miracle relationship—was anything but. I ended up using my power to get her fired, and then burning out and quitting myself a few months later.

Fast-forward twenty years, and I look back at that time as a turning point in my own leadership, not because of the success—but because of the failure. Acknowledging my contribution to the relational strife and the dark side of my ambition was an important step. I wish we could all learn from one relational failure and never experience that pain again. Every important relationship in life has the capacity to create deep connection or destructive conflict. Sometimes relationships have both.

As we near the end of our journey together, it's important to acknowledge the ways we have failed in our pursuit of the healthy relationships we desire so deeply, and how to fail forward into miracle moments in the future. If we mean what we feel, say what we mean, and do what we say and expect guaranteed success every time, we will be sorely disappointed—not only in other people but in ourselves. We can either stuff the pain of failure and keep repeating the same patterns that messed us up in the first place, or we can fail forward, choosing *curious, not condemning* as the gentle but truthful way to lean into the struggle.

Though we can't avoid failure, we can choose how we engage with our disappointment and grow through it. Failure can be an incredible teacher—in many ways, a better teacher than success. In the last chapter, we covered one reason why we won't always achieve the success we hope for—some people are simply not safe or open to continuing a relationship with us. Let's look at a few other reasons we might fail in our relationships, what happens afterward, and how we can learn, grow, and *experience miracle moments* even in failure.

Why We Fail

Mismatched expectations

When I was just beginning my work in ministry, I sat down with a more experienced leader whom I respected deeply for her compassion and teaching skills. I was just beginning to teach and write, and I wanted to know what lessons I could apply from her experience in ministry. Over mediocre fast-food salads, Kim told me this: "People generally think they can do more than they can actually do."

Without knowing Kim, you might interpret this as a harsh or even condemning statement. But in reality, Kim delivered this truth with such love and grace that it has stuck with me decades later. She knew that most of us have intentions that don't match our actions. We think we can do more, be more, and control more than we actually can. We think we can change our habits, change our relationships, and change our lives for the better without a real understanding of what it takes to truly transform them. And to top it off, we hold those same expectations for others.

What Kim knew was that mismatched expectations are inevitable. We believe others can be more than they can actually be. And if we hold tightly to unrealistic expectations—*or even realistic expectations that the other person doesn't align with*—our frustration and disappointment accumulate like a thick layer of dust, obscuring the original beauty and intent of the relationship.

- Mismatched expectations are why your friends sit you down and say, "He's just not that into you."
- Mismatched expectations are why you keep trying to impress your boss even though she never delivers the direction or support you really need.
- Mismatched expectations are why you feel like you are always trying to reignite the connection between you and your spouse and then don't understand why he isn't responding.

When we have mismatched expectations, we're operating from a belief system about how specific relationships should look and feel—the rock-bottom thoughts and feelings we believe to be true. We may not even be conscious of them. Many of us are unaware of those underlying assumptions until we experience a relational disappointment or failure. Sometimes that frustration is related to a boundary violation, but more often, people have not met our expectations in the way they behave or think. Belief systems reveal themselves in an inner narrative that goes something like this: *Husbands who really love their wives are romantic* or *Women aren't supposed to be that assertive* or *Best friends don't wait a day to respond to texts.* Most of the time, we have neither communicated our expectations to the other person nor done the deeper work of identifying and examining our belief systems to consider whether they are helpful, healthy, and accurate. We operate from belief systems about food, sex, money, gender roles, parenting, marriage, faith, our worth, and our impact. All of our behaviors, whether good or bad, generally stem from one of these rock-bottom beliefs.

While some beliefs are relatively innocuous and fairly easy to adjust (*Only guys take out the garbage!*), many are rooted in the inevitable wounds of childhood (regardless of how healthy our family is) or our life stories. When we haven't done the work necessary to heal from those wounds or better understand our stories, life can begin to feel dark and confusing. We find ourselves working out our issues with our father's authority by trying to be rigid with our boss. We attempt to work out issues related to our mother's manipulation by distancing ourselves from our wife's needs. We keep trying to prove our worth to our gorgeous, gregarious coworker just as we once did to our big brother, our first boyfriend, or our middle school frenemy. Even though those dynamics are rooted in what happened long ago, we keep living out the same patterns in our present relationships. Perhaps this is why the prophet Jeremiah said, "The heart is deceitful above all things and beyond cure. Who can understand it?" (Jeremiah 17:9, NIV).

On that happy note, you now understand why I put this chapter at the end of the book. If we started with that truth, we would all give up trying before we even begin! And it's true: The reaction of our hearts often feels beyond our own understanding. But it's not beyond God's understanding, and He offers us a way forward in the promise that we are His children, that His love is poured out on us, and that we can be made new.[1] If you keep failing at relationships, powerful belief systems from your past may be impacting your present and future.

Just as it's not always easy to know your own expectations in a relationship, it's even harder to know another person's. However, the more you apply the principles of healthy relationships that we've covered, such as becoming aware of your emotions and practice *curious, not condemning*, the more obvious those expectations will become. Two simple questions can help you understand and evaluate your mindset in any relationship:

- Given the length of time or commitment level of this relationship, do I have reasonable expectations, both for myself and the other person?
- Given the circumstances of this conflict, do I have reasonable expectations for myself and the other person?

Conversely, you can reflect on these questions on behalf of the other person. Are the expectations of your friend, spouse, or boss reasonable for both the relationship and the circumstance? If you sense that they aren't, you can work through the *say what you mean* process to try to uncover where you are not aligned. Relating to someone with mismatched expectations is like trying to balance on a seesaw. If both parties aren't willing to compromise, the relationship will remain unbalanced. Disappointment and resentment will creep in, undermining the vulnerability and strength of their connection.

Self-protection

We work on truly *meaning what we feel*. We work on truly *saying what we mean*. But when it comes to *doing what we say*—we fail and fail again. In addition to mismatched or unrealistic expectations, we may not follow through on doing what we say because we want to protect ourselves. We may lie about what we've done (or not done), go back on our word, or respond poorly due to fear or shame.

Because we'd rather avoid the truth or we lack the courage to speak it, we may compromise our integrity by choosing to tell a slippery lie rather than face a difficult conversation. We are hurt by an in-law at Thanksgiving dinner, but we don't want to make a big deal of it. So when that person asks if something is wrong during a break in the football game, we say "I'm fine" even though we've been ruminating about their comment for hours.

Our subtle lies reveal how duplicitous we can be with ourselves. On the one hand, no one wants to admit to lying. On the other hand, a *Psychology Today* article has observed, "Society often encourages and even rewards deception."[2] Most lying is not flamboyant storytelling—it's minimizing or embellishing; exaggerating or downplaying. Sometimes we lie to protect other people. Our spouse doesn't want to come to a work party, so we lie and say he had to watch the kids. This is where our fundamental law of *nice is bad* comes into play. Sometimes we lie to ourselves and others through avoidance. This is called a lie of omission—rather than add to or change the truth, we leave out parts of the truth.

Over time, as we avoid, minimize, embellish, exaggerate, or downplay our feelings, we may begin to lose our grip on what's real and true in our lives. Lying is a great short-term solution but a terrible long-term legacy. Usually underneath our lies is a deep fear of being rejected, a lack of courage around sticking to our boundaries, or a fear about engaging in conflict. But even when done out of kindness, lying is ultimately damaging because it erodes trust in those around us who don't know when we are saying what we really mean. And it erodes our trust in ourselves because it makes us more disconnected from what we like, want, and need. If either party in a relationship habitually lies—to the other person or to themselves—the relationship cannot grow to the levels of vulnerability and intimacy that our hearts crave.

> Lying is a great short-term solution but a terrible long-term legacy.

Secondary gain

When we fail in relationships—or when we refuse to back up our words with action—a secondary gain is in play. This is the benefit you get from staying stuck. For instance, Rich has an emotionally abusive wife, but the pain of imagining life without her feels harder than the pain of staying with her. Even though he complains about their relationship and has even threatened to leave unless she stops her abuse, he never follows through. Rich is settling for an unhappy life to avoid his worst-case scenario (WCS): his powerful fear that he will end up completely alone.

I've known many clients and friends who are unaware of the secondary gains that demotivate them from following through on what their own logic tells them to do. One of the most obvious examples of how this plays out is in a family with an adult child who has failed to launch. Even though both parents want to see the child move on, neither is willing to back up their talk with actual boundaries. Many times, the parents are unwilling to address the unhappiness and tension between the two of them. One or both spouses may even choose to be distracted by the adult child in order to avoid dealing with negative feelings about their partner. The young adult has a powerful secondary gain for remaining like a child as well—there is no need to get a job that will pay the rent! Of course, this is a black-and-white assessment of situations that are always gray. How we love, how we set boundaries, and how we follow through on those boundaries are rigorous tasks for all of us. But in order to love people into a place where they can truly flourish, we must have courage. When we take a *curious, not condemning* look at any relationships where we consistently don't follow through on our boundaries, we can gently address the secondary gain that may be holding us—and our loved ones—back.

Moving Forward from Failure

A great mentor of mine once said, "Relational failure is like gravity. It is a force you always have to exert pressure against in order to rise." I think the question is not *if* we will fail in a relationship, but what to do *when* we fail. Every day we encounter little failures—white lies, lack of follow-through, disengagement rather than cooperation. But there are also big failures—breakups and breaches that linger or are never resolved. Even if you handle your interactions perfectly, you might *still* have failed relationships because humans are complicated and mysterious. We can create linear patterns that generally hold true, but we can't create linear people who always act predictably. We can improve, we can grow, we can choose relationships that are healthy and life-giving— but we can't make those choices for other people.

So since failing at some point isn't optional, what then do we do with the kind of relational failure that can't be reconciled or restored? A reader recently asked me how to respond when a close friend rejected attempts at reconciliation:

> [Our friendship] tends to go smoothly for a time, and then she does not like me once again. I have not slept much over the past two nights. I think it is finally time to let it go and move forward, trusting in God's timing.
>
> I would love to reconcile, and I have tried, but I honestly believe it is time for me to do as you say—turn my heart to being thankful and grateful and let Him take care of that relationship. As much as I don't like to admit it, I don't like when people don't like me. . . . I tend to want to make it all good . . . and I have tried, but it never stays that way.

As I read this note, I could almost feel the tug within this woman— on the one hand to let it go; on the other, to continue trying to reconnect. I think that Christians in particular find it easy to hold on to a sense that if we "act like Christians," we can work it out. And yes, we'll explore the Bible's strong emphasis on healthy relationships in the corresponding Bible study for this book. But sometimes love *does* look like separation, especially when we acknowledge the reasons the relationship failed. If someone is not committed to honesty and growth, or is too tired, distracted, or selfish to work on the relationship, the best way to love them may be to create healthy distance and let it be. Some people move from being one of our closest friends to a more distant place in our relational circles. Sometimes it's because of them. Sometimes it's because of us. Most of the time we both contribute to the change. And when we come to grips with the reality of the relationship, regardless of what we wish were true, we must learn from and release the failure before we can move forward. Even if we do reconcile with that person later on, we will be unable to meet them with compassion and love if we are still holding on to what once was.

Miracles in Failure

Several years ago, I was assisting at a charity benefit for an organization in our community. During the reception, I spotted a well-known local leader—the retired CEO of a Fortune 100 company that had gone out of business just a few years prior. I had landed my very first "big girl" job out of college at that company, and to this day, I credit my ability to create a spreadsheet with formulas to my position there. (Heaven knows I didn't pick up that skill for the enjoyment of it.)

I stopped to introduce myself in the hallway. After we exchanged a few pleasantries, I said, "I want to thank you for your work in leadership. Your company gave me my very first job, and I'm so grateful for that experience."

I expected him to share some stories of the company's golden years or to reflect on what he was most proud of. I distinctly remember smiling up at him (he was quite tall) while waiting for his response, only to watch his face fall into a pained and sorrowful expression. He shook his head slowly. "Ah. It's such a shame what's happened. Such a shame." I had unintentionally stepped on an emotional land mine. Given the changing tides of culture and the economy, the failure of that company had felt inevitable to me. But to him, it was deeply personal and very real, even years later. The conversation stalled, but the moment has stuck with me.

In this small interaction, I got a glimpse into the kind of private grief so many of us carry about the failures in our lives—whether that's an estranged family member, a broken marriage, or a season of leadership that ended with great pain and relational fallout. Over the years, I've thought about that moment with the CEO frequently. I've thought about how easy it is to ascribe blame in failure, to long for what could have been, to retrace our steps and desperately look for the moment when we could have moved differently and avoided the pain.

Before that brief conversation in the hallway, where we were surrounded by beautiful, successful people doing beautiful, successful things, I would never have expected a man of such great renown—a man with a resumé star-studded with success after success, a loving marriage, healthy kids and grandkids, and a padded retirement account—to carry so much regret and sorrow. Somewhere deep in my soul, I knew that if a standout like him could fail, we can all fail. And if beautiful, successful people can't avoid inexplicable failings, no one is safe. No formula or technique can guarantee our victories in love and work. But we can allow those failures to teach us, to stretch us, to develop us in exquisite and important ways we can't learn any other way. Even in our loss, in other words, there is still gain. We often spend so much time fighting for a relationship to survive that we don't do the work needed after it dies. So when the dust clears and we find ourselves looking at a failure we can't fix or a relationship we can't bring back to life, we must find a way to keep going, to plant something new in that dead place in our lives.

Here are a few suggestions on how to live through the pain of a relational failure with integrity, and even find miracle moments within the process:

1. **Allow space to grieve.** Grieving is the normal reaction to loss. Often we think of it only as something we do after a loved one dies, but grief is the natural response to losses of all kinds—in friendship, in love, and in work. When we must let go of something or someone we cherish, we experience a complex set of emotions—from anger to regret, from guilt to anxiety. We often swing wildly from one emotion to the next as our hearts try to process the emptiness we feel. If we were the ones to end the relationship, we may be surprised and confused when we find ourselves overwhelmed by our emotional reaction to the loss.

   Even if the healthiest choice was to move on from the job or the relationship, it doesn't change the reality of our pain. In that situation, we may be tempted to stuff any feelings of regret or sadness to prove to ourselves that we made the right decision. But good decisions can still be excruciatingly hard. Good decisions that bring on relational failures—whether that's what you wanted or not—are still painful. And we can't control or rush grief. It's like the wind—it blows in unexpected directions. We can fight the wind—or we can move with it. To move with our grief is to allow space to feel it, even when it's painful. It's listening to our heart and acknowledging what we've lost— whether a sense of identity, a future, or the parts of that person you liked or loved. When we make space to grieve, we can also recognize the ripple effects of the loss, which can result in fallout in other relationships and plans. When we feel stuck in the hurt, a trusted counselor or spiritual director can come alongside us in our grief to help us make space in constructive ways.

In a recent season of transition, I was surprised to discover the miracle moments in failure. During my own struggles, I reached out to several colleagues to seek wisdom and direction. I was shocked to discover that each of these friends had experienced a deep relational failure of their own. In our shared pain, there was a miracle moment. Our mutual vulnerability in failure created a deep connection. And in that connection, I found the courage to keep failing forward.

A trusted pastor once told me it took him over seven years to forgive after a painful job transition. His admission stopped me short because this man acts and loves more like Jesus than just about anyone I know. Whenever a loss or relational failure feels particularly hard, I remember my friend.

We need to trust our grief. When we make space to feel the painful parts of the loss, healing will come.

10 QUESTIONS TO USE TO LEARN FROM FAILURE

1. What do I miss?
2. What dreams do I need to release for now?
3. What unrealistic expectations did I have of myself?
4. What unrealistic expectations did I have of the other person?
5. What do I now know is essential for me, moving forward?
6. What do I need to acknowledge is unfinished?
7. Who do I need to forgive?
8. How do I want to be different from this?
9. How do I want to be stronger from this?
10. How do I now define success in relationships?

2. Recognize and release expectations. My counseling supervisor used to say, "If you can forgive your parents by age thirty, you are in the healthy range of humanity." Whether we've been hurt by our parents or someone else close to us, we must recognize and release expectations—both of ourselves and of those who failed us—so we can learn from our failures. By recognizing our expectations of what we wanted another person to be in our lives, we learn what's important to us and what we might do differently moving forward. When we find ourselves knocked out emotionally, we are in the best position to honestly answer the question, "What's worth fighting for?"

When we put up healthy boundaries and someone we love responds with guilt, demands, or abandonment, we can acknowledge that we had a healthy expectation the person could not meet. When we haven't put up boundaries or communicated them clearly, or if we realize we had unrealistic expectations for how that person should meet our needs, we can dust ourselves off, learn from our mistakes, and move forward. The only worthless failure is an unexamined failure.

> The only worthless failure is an unexamined failure.

When we review the course of a failed relationship and treat the strengths and weaknesses we brought to it with gentleness and curiosity, we have begun allowing something good to be born out of loss. It doesn't happen immediately, or even quickly. But one step at a time, tender shoots of new life begin to spring out of the barren place of loss. It won't be quick and it won't be easy—but it will happen.

3. Recognize and release unfinished business. Failure brings hidden losses, such as the loss of the future we imagined and worked toward. No one plans for relational failures. Nobody enters into a marriage, a business venture, or a friendship thinking, *This is going to be awesome for years and then completely fall apart! We are going to pledge our hearts to each other and then act like strangers years later!* No. Failure can come unexpectedly and fiercely like a car accident, or long and painfully like cancer. Either way, there is always unfinished business, whether words that weren't said, promises that weren't kept, experiences that weren't enjoyed, or wounds that weren't healed. In fact, it requires as much effort to release unfinished business as it does to release the relationship itself.

One of the ways that you can reframe what feels incomplete is by viewing your life as a relay rather than an individual race. Hebrews 12:1 says, "Let us run with perseverance the race marked out for us" (NIV). What we thought would be a marathon may have been only a sprint. We carried the baton for a season, and then it was time to pass it on. That doesn't mean our race is over, but it does mean that one leg has come to an end. Rather than looking back with regret at what we didn't finish or accomplish in the relationship, we can trust that the baton was passed at just the right moment and that our race is now taking us in a new direction. Our unfinished business can become someone else's next goal. When we trust that God is at work, we can release and entrust that which is undone into His hands, hopeful that the next person will pick up where we left off.

4. **Be human.** As human beings, we have been given an incredible capacity for imagination and planning. We have been given the capacity to hope for love, and to act on love. And with all of that great expectation comes great risk: To be human is also to fail. Erich Fromm, a renowned psychologist in the mid-1900s, said,

"There is hardly any activity, any enterprise, which is started with such tremendous hopes and expectations, and yet, which fails so regularly, as love."[3] When failure comes, we have to decide if we will allow those we held in high esteem to be human. We have to decide if we will allow ourselves to be human—in our failures, our frailty, and our pain. If we do, we will discover one of humanity's greatest gifts—the ability to rise again. It is only in brokenness that we discover our resilience. It is only in death that we discover resurrection.

When you rise to try again (and you will), you'll discover that resilience has shaped something new in you. Perhaps you have the courage to be a truth teller when you used to be a reality avoider. Perhaps you've grown gentler and more compassionate when you used to be hard-charging and aggressive. If you'll enter fully into the sharpening that follows relational failure, you will develop resilience in the direction you've been missing.

A friend of mine said it this way after a career failure with painful relational fallout haunted him for years:

> I had to learn to give myself permission to be angry. Without letting myself be angry, I couldn't get to the part where release is possible. Even though as a pastor I knew redemption is real, I didn't know it for myself. Now that I'm years outside of [the failure], I know that redemption is possible, and that even gratitude for it happening is possible. I've had to choose to own my part and see the experience as a learning and growing opportunity. I had to release the people who hurt me, and without necessarily seeing them acknowledge or repent of their part in the failing. But I realized I couldn't move forward and still hold on to all that pain, waiting for them to come around. I was only hurting myself.

Failure is a great catalyst for either bitterness and anger or resiliency and compassion. You may not have chosen this failure. But the choice of what you do with it is yours.

〰〰〰

Questions to Consider

1. How do you handle failure in yourself? In others?

2. When you experience failure, how easy is it to forgive yourself? Others?

3. What is something you've learned through failure that you would not have learned otherwise?

CHAPTER 12

INTEGRITY IN ACTION

᭺᭺᭺᭺᭺

If you are here unfaithfully with us, you're causing terrible damage.
RUMI, THIRTEENTH-CENTURY POET

I BELIEVE THE SACRED and courageous work of aligning our souls—of becoming people who *mean what we feel*, *say what we mean*, and *do what we say*—positions us for miracle moments of all kinds.

Remember Katie and Tripp, whose battle over the way he used his cell phone led to an argument in my office? Because they accepted my invitation to be introspective, I got to witness a miracle moment between them. Rather than digging in their heels, each was willing to dig deeper into the emotions and past experiences that were creating a breach between them. They were then able to set healthy boundaries and trust each other more.

Several weeks after that conversation, I officiated at Katie and Tripp's wedding. In a beautiful backyard ceremony, surrounded by an intimate circle of family and friends, the couple added a few promises as they exchanged the more traditional wedding vows. As Tripp held Katie's hands in his, he said:

I promise to always listen to you, even when we disagree,
and understand that love is "I feel differently" and not "you're
wrong."

We all laughed (especially the couples who'd been married for a while!). Tripp's promise was a commitment to choose the miracle with Katie— to yield to each other and then fight to get what was inside to the outside, to fight for compromise and apologies and trying again.

Then Katie made this promise:

I vow to always be honest and to have open conversations,
even when I'm having a bad day.

Although I love traditional vows, I loved these add-ons Tripp and Katie made to their ceremony. In their vows, they owned their humanity. They claimed their individual propensities to want to be right, to want to shut down, to want to dig in rather than lean in. That level of self-awareness and self-expression in the middle of their promises was both endearing and empowering.

Katie and Tripp had struggled through enough conflict while dating to know that tough conversations can lead to deeper connection. And they knew that those conversations were so important that, right at the beginning of their marriage, it was worth making promises to continue them.

Contentment and depth in our relationships come not so much from the times when things go right, but from what we do when things go wrong. The joyful, easy times are made sweeter by the arguments we've resolved, the hardships we've shared, and the push and pull, the give-and-take of becoming people who can acknowledge hurt, resolve differences, and live out committed love in our families, friendships, and communities.

Miracle moments happen every day, within us and between us. They happen as we learn to trust and honor our emotions. Miracle moments occur as we begin to understand what it means to be self-defined individuals with a non-anxious presence. They come about when we lean into our relationships with curiosity and hope. Miracle moments are possible when we commit to seeking understanding, common ground, and restoration in conflict. They show up when we know what healthy boundaries are and honor those boundaries in ourselves and others. Miracle moments happen in the seconds after a conflict erupts when we choose to fight for vulnerability and rebuilding.

And for Katie and Tripp, a miracle moment served as a promise of what their marriage could be.

The Lasting Legacy of Miracle Moments

Two days after Katie and Tripp's wedding, I was exchanging texts with my neighbor and new best friend, Claudia. It was the spring of 2020, and Covid-19 had changed our lives drastically. One silver lining had been the new friendships we'd made with our neighbors, including Claudia and Steve, a couple in their sixties who lived directly across the street from us.

At our previous socially distanced neighborhood gathering, Claudia had told me her disappointment that her wedding anniversary surprise for Steve had been foiled by the pandemic. Their forty-fifth wedding anniversary was coming up, and she had pulled out all the stops for a vow renewal—a caterer, a band, a full-on party. Knowing that those fun festivities were now forbidden in this season, we conspired together to plan a simplified but meaningful event to make their anniversary special. I promised to come over and share a blessing when they renewed their vows.

The next evening, Dave and I walked across the street to the back-yard celebration, this one featuring plastic glasses of champagne so we could toast Claudia and Steve. With their daughter's family standing around them and other family members watching on FaceTime, I asked Claudia and Steve what they had learned in their first ten years of marriage and what they'd learned during their last ten. Claudia remembered how she grew up in that first year of marriage, discovering what it really meant to share life together. Steve recalled how their first ten years had been full of suffering and hardship—and that deciding to rely on and lean into each other brought them through that and led to the sweetness of their last ten years of marriage.

And just as Katie and Tripp had held one another's hands as they recited their vows, Claudia and Steve turned and held each other's hands as I recited a blessing to celebrate their forty-five years of faithfulness:

> May the years of choosing to lean in rather than distance,
> to forgive rather than resent, to yield rather than resist be
> rewarded with a trust and delight in one another that make
> the day you first began your marriage pale in comparison.

Love is found in moments like these. Love isn't formed on stages—it's formed *in* stages. Love shows up in the backyard of life, where we play together, talk together, fight together, and make up together.

It's easy to get drawn into the young love of Katie and Tripp, fresh in their relationship and full of hope. But the rich love of Claudia and Steve, a love that has weathered hardship, raising children, and the changing seasons of life—a love with deep roots and strong ties—offers us all a vision of what can be. If Katie and Tripp are the sapling, Claudia and Steve are the oak: strong; rooted; providing shelter, shade, and rest for those who are looking for stability and hope.

I opened this final chapter with the words of the thirteenth-century poet, Rumi: "If you are here unfaithfully with us, you're causing terrible damage." Living faithfully doesn't mean living perfectly; it means living with honesty and vulnerability. If, on the other hand, you are living your life in neutral, you are robbing the rest of us of the fullness of who you are. If you are shutting down your heart and coasting through life, you are exchanging depth and delight for distance and disappointment. If you are living from anything but the fullness of your heart and mind, you are shrinking not just from your own life but from the lives of those who need you to show up with integrity:

> *If you are here unfaithfully with us,*
> *You're causing terrible damage.*

The poem goes on:

> *If you've opened your loving to God's love,*
> *You're helping people you don't know and have never seen.*

When you open your life to loving, you open yourself up to others. And that requires vulnerability. It can be painful and hard. You may be rejected or betrayed or abandoned or misunderstood. But unless you open up, you will also miss out on what may be waiting for you on the other side of vulnerability: Connection. Joy. Meaning. Legacy.

After I delivered Claudia and Steve's blessing, their grandson piped up on FaceTime: "Can I share something?"

At the tender age of nine, Aidan said, "If it weren't for you, I wouldn't be here."

Steve chuckled. "That's literally true." And it is.

The legacy of Claudia and Steve's love is expressed in grandchildren, but also in much more. Because when you and I are faithful and true, we are impacting people we will never know. The cumulative effect of our relationships over time—the way we yield, grow, soften, strengthen—can ripple out, bringing healing and life to generations to come. But if you and I live unfaithfully in our one beautiful, wild life, we are doing terrible damage.

The world needs you to show up for your life. To open up and learn how to listen to your own heart, to find the words to cover and cross the inevitable breaches in your love and work. The world needs you to know who you are and what you are worth, and to express that with all the courage you can find. The world needs you to have faith that you can start again after failing, that you can love again after heartbreak, that you can joke again after fighting.

One of my favorite lyrics comes from the Christmas carol "O Holy Night," and it feels like the perfect summary of our call to action together.

Truly He taught us to love one another
His law is love and His gospel is peace

The law of love has no bounds. It is the law that draws us back to one another, that allows us to express ourselves from a place of our own belovedness while creating safety for others to do the same.

The gospel of peace comes in the form of alignment—of bringing the inner world in line with the outer; of trusting that words spoken in truth may hurt but to hold them in is to bring even greater harm. The law of love and the gospel of peace allow us to move toward one another with the hope of greater compassion and meaning, even when it means disrupting or dismantling anything less than true.

May the law of love, the gospel of peace, and the boldness of hope be the compass for your path. May you choose courageous vulnerability with the people you love. May you pause long enough in conflict to choose the miracle moment. And may you never stop growing into the fullness of the person you were created to be.

∧∧∧∧∧

Questions to Consider

1. What would growing in integrity look like for you in this season?

2. When you think about the three parts of this book—*meaning what you feel, saying what you mean*, and *doing what you say*—which area most needs attention in your life?

3. As you finish this book, what relationship do you want to intentionally work on? What step can you take in the next week to begin creating space for a miracle moment with that person?

Acknowledgments

WRITING A BOOK IN A PANDEMIC—not recommended. However, the belief and encouragement of those around me are what brought this book into being, and I am so grateful for the extraordinary sacrifices made to allow me to focus and connect to this message.

To Jenni Burke and the team at Illuminate: Thank you for the way you've come alongside me in such a crucial and sensitive time in my life and career. Your wisdom, gentleness, and compassion are evident in every conversation and email exchange. Let's celebrate in Tuscany someday!

To Jan, Sarah, Kim, Kara, Jillian, and the whole team at Tyndale: You've been my champions since the beginning, and it's been a joy to partner together through the twists and turns of this publishing journey. Your faith in me and my message is beyond compare. Sarah, I'll always cherish our conversation that unlocked this book's introduction and the way you shared at sales conference. That was my favorite miracle moment so far.

To AJ, Tyler, Jenna, Melissa, and Matt: You guys are the best team! Every one of you has sprinkled a little magic in my work in a way that has not only helped our people but also helped me. There's no way I would even keep my head on straight without you people, and you know it (and stick with me anyway!).

To Courtney, Phil, and the RightNow Media crew: What I love even more than fourteen-hour filming days (!) are your love for the message of the gospel and your creative, humble, confident attitudes. It's always a joy to work together, and I'm grateful you've taken a chance on another project together!

To Carrie, Fran, and Melissa (again!): A girl couldn't ask for a better tribe. Thanks for putting up with me, letting me vent, pointing me back to Jesus, and always having more faith in me than I have in myself. You've taught me how miracle moments truly do move us closer to one another in ways I would have never believed if I hadn't experienced them.

To my church families across the country: Thank you for taking me in as your own, whether it was one Sunday service or several. Your hunger for God's Word and responsiveness to the gospel has encouraged and deepened my own faith in a way that is its own miracle. Thank you.

To my kids, Charlie, Cameron, Desmond: From the moment you were born, I knew my understanding of love was forever altered. But what I didn't know was how much fun, delight, and pure admiration I would have watching you grow. May you always stay curious as God directs your path, and may you grow in your own understanding of healthy relationships.

To Dave, my greatest source of love (and miracle moments!) in my life: Your anchored and unshakable faith in me and my calling has kept me from all kinds of danger and derailing. Thank you for your nonstop enthusiasm, your love of daily life, and your way of always sending me out—and welcoming me back home. I'm particularly grateful for you letting me escape and write at hotels even during this crazy lockdown.

Words cannot capture how dramatically my life is changed because of the grace of Jesus Christ. It is only through Him and in relationship with Him that I've experienced the inside-out miracle of growing in love, in faith, and in courage in all my relationships. I'll repeat the words of the apostle Paul that have inspired my journey here and beyond:

> I consider my life worth nothing to me; my only aim is to finish the race and complete the task the Lord Jesus has given me—the task of testifying to the good news of God's grace.
> ACTS 20:24, NIV

And of course you, my readers: May the words of this book inspire a deeper curiosity and confidence in the power of miracle moments in your relationships, and may you discover a more meaningful life through the exact time and place you've been planted to grow.

Notes

CHAPTER 2: THE MAKING OF A MIRACLE

1. Stephanie Vozza, "The Science behind Why Breaking a Habit Is So Hard," *Fast Company*, June 20, 2016, https://www.fastcompany.com/3060892/the-science -behind-why-breaking-a-bad-habit-is-so-hard.

2. Oliver Burkeman, "The Incredibly Annoying Psychology of Christmas Holiday Regression," *Guardian*, December 20, 2013, https://www.theguardian.com/news /oliver-burkeman-s-blog/2013/dec/20/psychology-christmas-holiday-family -regression.

3. Elizabeth Gilbert, *Big Magic: Creative Living beyond Fear* (New York: Riverhead, 2015), 8.

4. "What Did the Word Nice Use to Mean?," Dictionary.com, accessed October 15, 2020, https://www.dictionary.com/e/nice-guys/.

5. There is no such thing as the Nice Disorder in any diagnostic manual, but this disorder is very real in my world. Obviously, when you are experiencing thoughts or behaviors that are impacting your ability to work, keep up with your basic daily needs, or form relationships, please seek professional help in the form of a doctor, psychologist, or counselor.

6. Jordan B. Peterson, *12 Rules for Life: An Antidote to Chaos* (Toronto: Random House Canada, 2018), 36.

7. Geneen Roth, *Lost and Found: Unexpected Revelations about Food and Money* (New York: Viking Penguin, 2011), 194.

8. Qing Li, *Forest Bathing: How Trees Can Help You Find Health and Happiness* (New York: Viking, 2018), 64, 102.

9. Pelin Kesebir, "Virtues: Irreplaceable Tools to Cultivate Your Well-Being," Center for Healthy Minds, University of Wisconsin–Madison, accessed October 16, 2010, https://centerhealthyminds.org/join-the-movement/virtues-irreplaceable-tools-to -cultivate-your-well-being.

CHAPTER 3: POSITIONING YOURSELF FOR A MIRACLE

1. Nicole Unice, "A Visit with the Bride," *Today's Christian Woman*, June 2012, https://www.todayschristianwoman.com/articles/2012/june/visitwithbride.html.
2. Definition adapted from Edwin Friedman, *A Failure of Nerve: Leadership in the Age of the Quick Fix* (New York: Seabury Books, 2007), 151.
3. Mark Batterson, *The Circle Maker* (Grand Rapids, MI: Zondervan, 2011), chapter 15.
4. Ecclesiastes 3:11.
5. Saul McLeod, "Maslow's Hierarchy of Needs," Simply Psychology, March 20, 2020, https://www.simplypsychology.org/maslow.html.
6. Brené Brown, *Rising Strong: How the Ability to Reset Transforms the Way We Live, Love, Parent, and Lead* (New York: Random House, 2015), 82.
7. Roger Fisher, William Ury, and Robert Patton, *Getting to Yes: Negotiating Agreement without Giving In,"* rev. ed. (New York: Penguin, 2011), 5.
8. Fisher, Ury, and Patton, *Getting to Yes*, 4–5.

CHAPTER 4: WHY FEELINGS ARE SO HARD TO FIND

1. For more on how your temperament impacts your decision-making and relationships, you can access a free assessment using the Myers-Briggs Type Indicator at 16personalities.com.
2. Lauri Nummenmaa et al., "Bodily Maps of Emotions," *Proceedings of the National Academy of Sciences* 111, no. 2 (January 14, 2014): 646–51, https://doi.org/10.1073/pnas.1321664111.
3. See chapter 4 in my book *The Struggle Is Real* (Carol Stream, IL: Tyndale House, 2018).

CHAPTER 5: TRUE YOU: HOW TO BECOME MORE SELF-AWARE

1. Kerry Patterson et al., *Crucial Conversations: Tools for Talking When the Stakes Are High* (New York: McGraw-Hill, 2012), 117–36.
2. Patterson, *Crucial Conversations*, 117.

CHAPTER 6: SEEK TO UNDERSTAND

1. Brené Brown, *Rising Strong: How the Ability to Reset Transforms the Way We Live, Love, Parent, and Lead* (New York: Random House, 2015), 19.
2. P. M. Forni, *Choosing Civility: The Twenty-Five Rules of Considerate Conduct* (New York: St. Martin's Griffin, 2002), 106.

CHAPTER 7: SEEK THE COMMON GOOD

1. Brené Brown, *Dare to Lead* (New York: Random House, 2018), 10.
2. "Eleanor Roosevelt Biography," website of the Franklin D. Roosevelt Presidential Library and Museum, accessed October 20, 2020, https://www.fdrlibrary.org/er-biography.
3. Karl Albrecht, "The (Only) 5 Fears We All Share," *Psychology Today*, March 22,

2012, https://www.psychologytoday.com/gb/blog/brainsnacks/201203/the-only
-5-fears-we-all-share.

4. Kerry Patterson et al., *Crucial Conversations: Tools for Talking When Stakes Are High* (New York: McGraw-Hill Education, 2012), 60.

5. Gayle King, "The Gayle King Interview with R. Kelly," CBS News, March 9, 2019, https://www.cbsnews.com/news/r-kelly-interview-full-coverage-of-the-gayle-king -interview-with-r-kelly-on-cbs-2019-03-08/.

6. Andy Crouch, "What's So Great about 'The Common Good'?" *Christianity Today*, November 2012, http://andy-crouch.com/articles/whats_so_great_about_the _common_good.6.

CHAPTER 8: SEEK RESTORATION

1. "Jean Paul Samputu," The Forgiveness Project, https://www.theforgivenessproject .com/stories/jean-paul-samputu/.

2. Jean Paul Samputu, "Forgiveness: The Unpopular Weapon," TedxHagueAcademy, September 9, 2013, https://www.youtube.com/watch?v=gRVjfRXt1Mc.

3. "Jean Paul Samputu," The Forgiveness Project.

4. "Jean Paul Samputu," The Forgiveness Project.

5. Duncan Haughey, "A Brief History of SMART Goals," Project Smart, December 13, 2014, https://www.projectsmart.co.uk/brief-history-of-smart-goals.php.

6. Haughey, "Brief History."

7. "Tell Me the Truth," words by Steffany Gretzinger, Amanda Cook, and Bobby Strand. Copyright © 2017 by Bethel Music Publishing (ASCAP) / Steffany Gretzinger Publishing. All rights reserved.

CHAPTER 9: BOUNDARIES: SHAPING YOUR YES AND NO

1. John Townsend and Henry Cloud, *Boundaries* (Grand Rapids, MI: Zondervan, 1992).

2. Anthony Bouchard, "Trees Have a Defense Mechanism against Being Eaten," LabRoots, September 23, 2016, https://www.labroots.com/trending/plants-and -animals/4153/trees-defense-mechanism-eaten.

3. Priyanka Pulla, "Why Do Humans Grow Up So Slowly? Blame the Brain," *Science*, August 25, 2014, https://www.sciencemag.org/news/2014/08/why-do-humans -grow-so-slowly-blame-brain.

4. A full definition of *gaslighting* appears in the next chapter. Simply put, gaslighting is a tactic used by someone who wants to make you second-guess or doubt your own reality.

5. For more help with boundaries and boundary issues, visit nicoleunice.com /boundaries.

CHAPTER 10: WHEN IT DOESN'T GET BETTER

1. Matthew 10:16, NIV.

2. John 5:6, NIV.

3. Luke 15:11-32.

4. Keiana Smith-McDowel, "Depression Risk Factor Can Be 'Contagious,' Study Finds," National Alliance on Mental Illness, April 30, 2013, https://www.nami .org/About-NAMI/NAMI-News/2013/Depression-Risk-Factor-Can-Be -Contagious-Study.

5. Randy A. Sansone and Lori A. Sansone, "Personality Disorders: A Nation-Based Perspective on Prevalence," *Innovations in Clinical Neuroscience* 8, no. 4 (April 2011): 13–18, https://www.ncbi.nlm.nih.gov/pubmed/21637629.

6. First coined by Susan Forward and Donna Frazier in *Emotional Blackmail: When the People in Your Life Use Fear, Obligation, and Guilt to Manipulate You* (New York: HarperCollins, 1997). The acronym FOG stands for fear, obligation, and guilt.

7. Dana Morningstar, *Out of the Fog: Moving from Confusion to Clarity after Narcissistic Abuse* (Mason, MI: Morningstar Media, 2017), 25.

CHAPTER 11: FAILING FORWARD

1. If you'd like to explore belief systems and how to better understand your story, check out my book *The Struggle Is Real*, where I cover these topics more deeply.

2. Allison Kornet, "The Truth about Lying," *Psychology Today*, May 1, 1997, https://www.psychologytoday.com/us/articles/199705/the-truth-about-lying.

3. Erich Fromm, *The Art of Loving* (New York: HarperPerennial, 2006), 4.

About the Author

NICOLE UNICE is a pastor, counselor, and leadership coach who facilitates environments of safety and vulnerability so that leaders and teams can courageously identify obstacles keeping them from maximum potential. Her expertise in both individual and systems health and her skill as a coach and facilitator equip her to help organizations identify their actual problems and discover innovative solutions.

Nicole encourages her clients to work toward understanding themselves in order to effectively lead others. She employs a broad range of approaches from both counseling and leadership development, and is known for facilitating innovative thinking that brings individuals and teams to breakthrough insights. Working with Nicole, leaders can expect to be both inspired and challenged to think deeper and work harder to achieve their preferred outcomes.

As a sought-after speaker on stages of all sizes, Nicole has a down-to-earth style that allows even the largest gathering to feel conversational. Nicole is the author of several books focused on spiritual transformation and is a featured speaker through RightNow Media and Punchline, and is the host of the *Let's Be Real* podcast, a conversation about healthy relationships with ourselves and one another.

She holds degrees from the College of William and Mary and from Gordon-Conwell Theological Seminary.

Nicole and her husband, Dave, live in Richmond, Virginia, with their three children and two pups. Discover more at nicoleunice.com.

It's time to transform your relationships at home, in love, and at work.
Are you ready for your miracle moment?

The Miracle Moment Discover the moment in every conversation that can change the whole relationship. Popular speaker Nicole Unice helps you discover the practical tools, words, and boundaries that will transform conflict into connection—even when you're tempted to shut up, blow up, or give up.

The Miracle Moment DVD Experience Nicole shines on video in this six-session series, teaching you how to recognize and respond to miracle moments and transform the relationships you have into the ones you really want.

Also available through online streaming at www.rightnowmedia.org.

The Miracle Moment Participant's Guide A six-session workbook designed to accompany *The Miracle Moment DVD Experience*, created for group or individual use.

Visit Nicole online at nicoleunice.com.

CP1686